Bill Mauldin's Army

PRESIDIO

Dedicated to the World War II staffs of the *45th Division News* and the Mediterranean *Stars and Stripes*.

Reprinted 1983 by Presidio Press
505 B San Marin Dr., Suite 300, Novato, CA 94945-1340
This edition printed 1995

Library of Congress Cataloging in Publication Data

Mauldin, Bill, 1921—
    Bill Mauldin's army.

    Originally published: New York: Sloan, 1949.
    1. World War, 1939–1945—Caricatures and cartoons.
2. American wit and humor, Pictorial. I. Title.
D745.2.M318 1983   940.53'0207   82-23141
ISBN 0-89141-180-1 hardcover
        0-89141-159-3 paperback

Typography and format designed by Leonard W. Blizard
Manufactured in the United States of America

Introduction

I wish I could do this book over again. It was put together some thirty-odd years ago, soon after World War II, so I claim youth and inexperience as an alibi. My problem is that the cartoons, which I drew during my five years of Army service from 1940 to 1945, should have been arranged in the book in chronological order. Instead, for some reason I chose to group them more or less by subject (discomfort, rank, weather, food, etc.) and in two broad categories (training and overseas).

Had everything appeared in proper sequence, the discerning student of ancient military history could have easily followed changes in the Army and in the characters themselves. As it is, older readers who remember Willie and Joe will be confused by early, clean-shaven versions of those two worthies popping up alongside later portraits of them in rags with their beards in full flower.

Confusion will be compounded by the fact that I switched the soldiers' names in mid-career. During training Joe was a smart-assed Choctaw Indian with a hooked nose and Willie was his red-necked straight man. As they matured overseas during the stresses of shot, shell, and K-rations, and grew whiskers because shaving water was scarce in mountain fox-holes, for some reason Joe seemed to become more of a Willie and Willie more of a Joe.

I've begged Presidio Press to let me set things straight or to include a razor blade with each book so the serious reader can do the job himself, but they have refused on both counts, claiming authenticity in reprinting an early work takes prece-dence over all else. I beg *your* indulgence.

Bill Mauldin

Garrison Life, Training,

This first part covers the period from mid-1940 to the actual war overseas. The material is grouped by subject matter, not chronologically, and therefore an old-fashioned flat helmet or a Springfield rifle (which were the style in 1940 when stovepipes simulated mortars and the jeep was a new discovery) will pop up in drawings from time to time on the same pages with more modern equipment.

and Maneuvers

Bus Stop

"Who's brushin' my teeth?"

"Oh, by the way—clean sheets today."

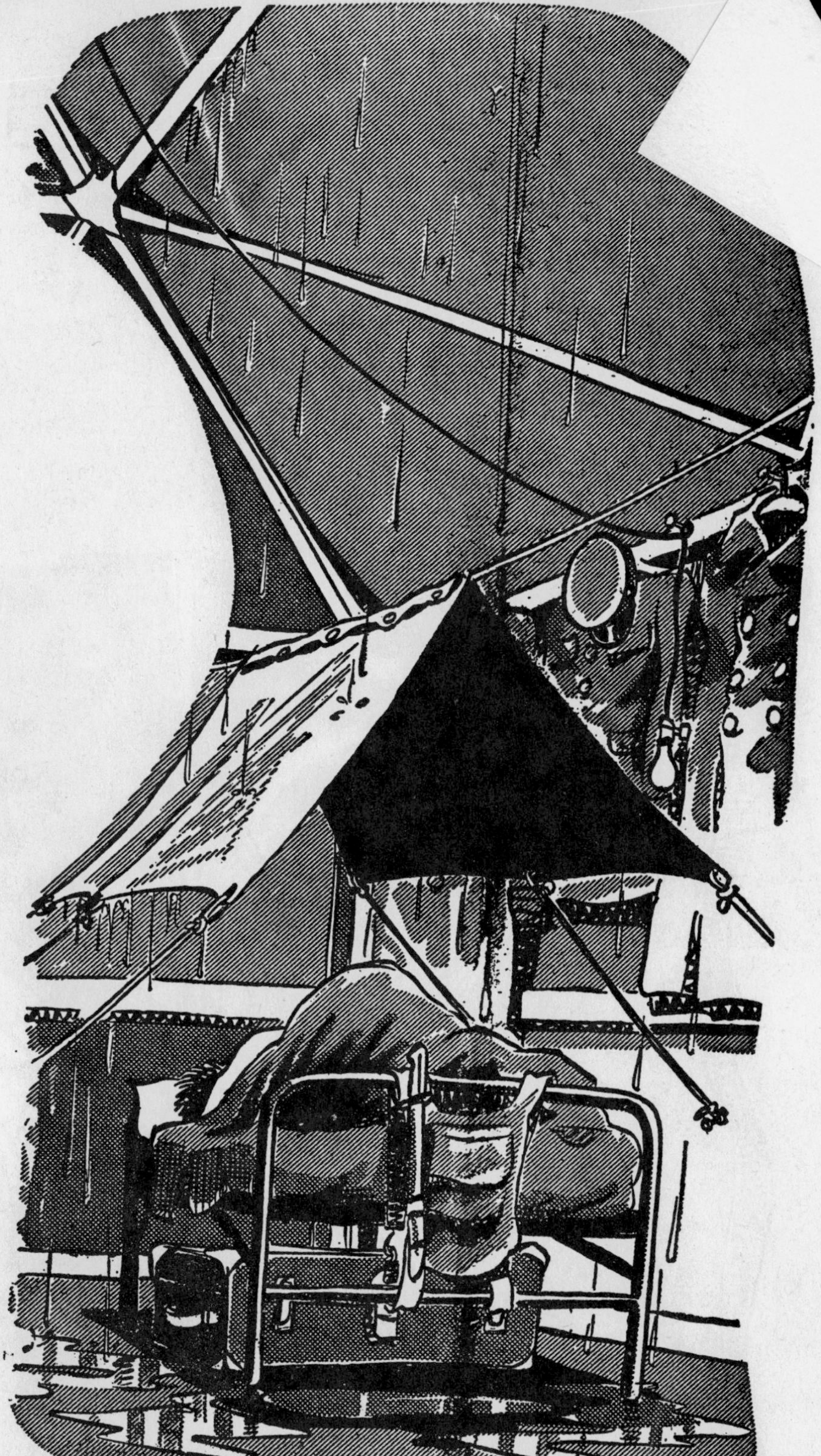

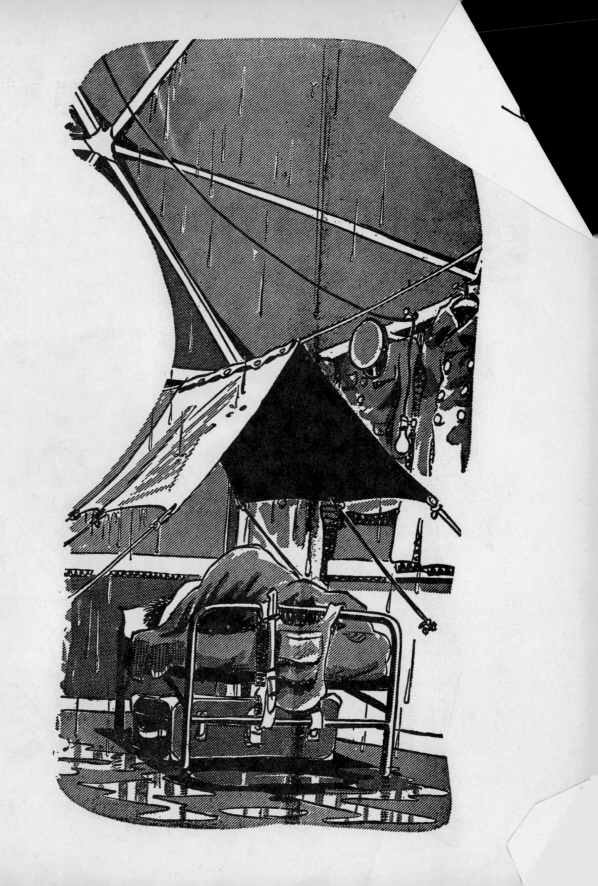

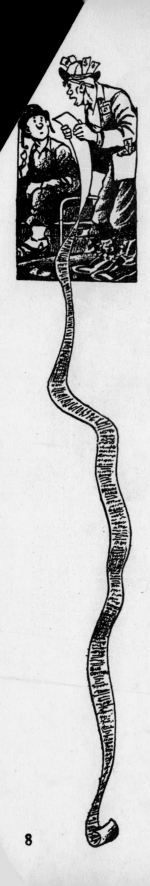

"Why, yes, I'm goin' to th' PX
—why?"

"You kin come down now. I don't think it's clogged
any more."

"Comp'ny A left a shower runnin'
last night."

"There seems t' be mixed feelings about Tschaikovsky . . .

and hillbilly music."

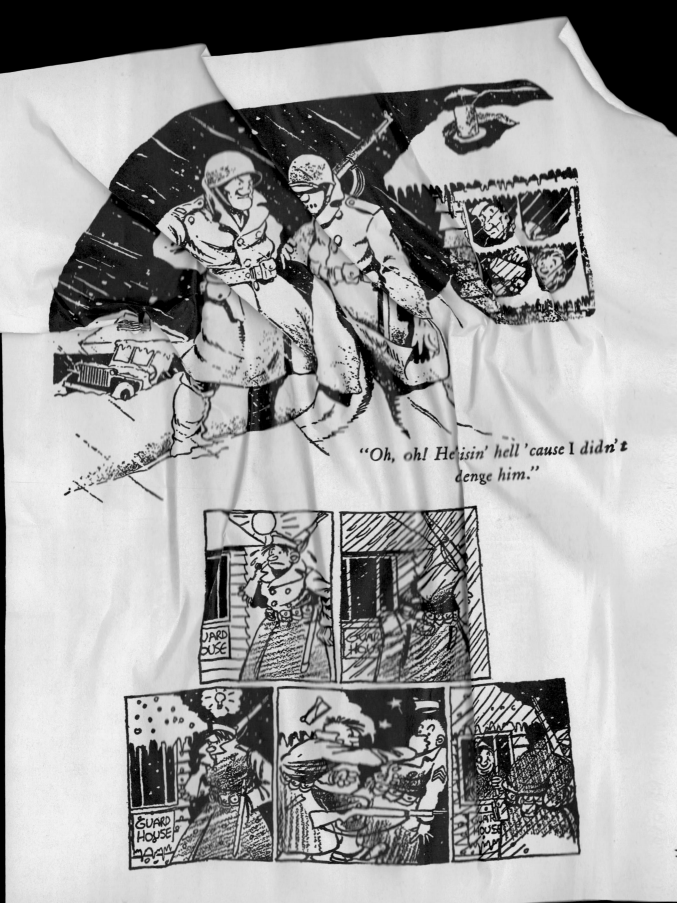

"Oh, oh! He'isin' hell 'cause I didn't
denge him."

*"Sir, it is your order that all persons crossin' this post
will dismount an' be reckanized."*

*"What are ya standin' there gawkin' about? Go on out
an' start walkin' post number three."*

"Why, Colonel Gilhooley!"

"Pass, friend."

'Come out an' look for yaself.'

"*Another inspection. Must have lemon pie today.*"

"Awright, let's settle it this way—th' man what took th' next to th' last chop has to go fill th' plate."

"Hmm. Johnson, your stew is still bad. The boys seemed to like Oswald's corn fritters okay, but they're having to put sugar in Pete's custard."

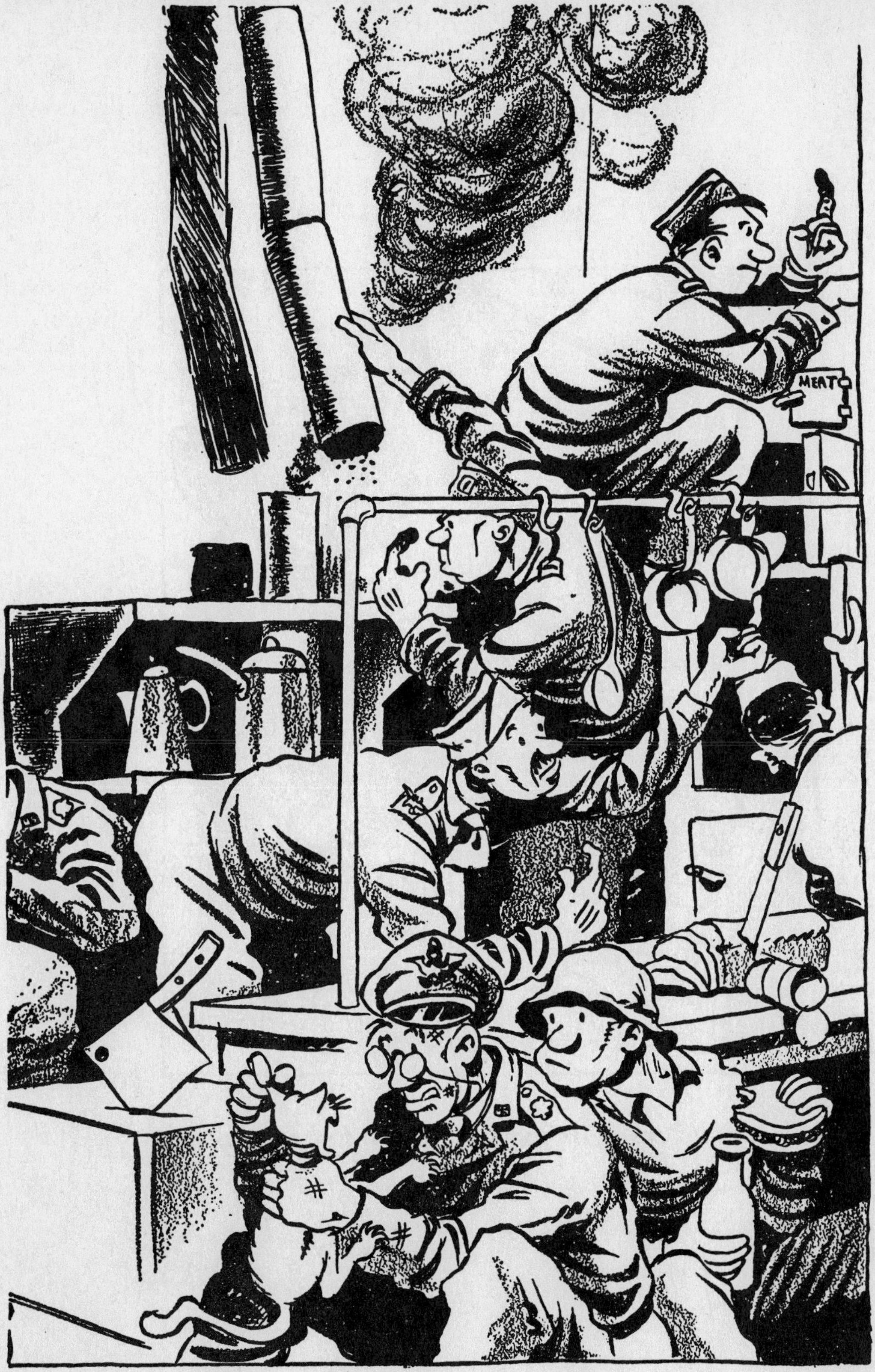
MEAT

"That's my case. Ain't you never heard of perfessional ethics?"

"Sergeant Fitch sent me to take his place. He's busy."

"Who's been talking to this man?"

"You're in bad shape, man! Run over to your barracks, get your stuff together, and be back in five minutes ready for the ambulance."

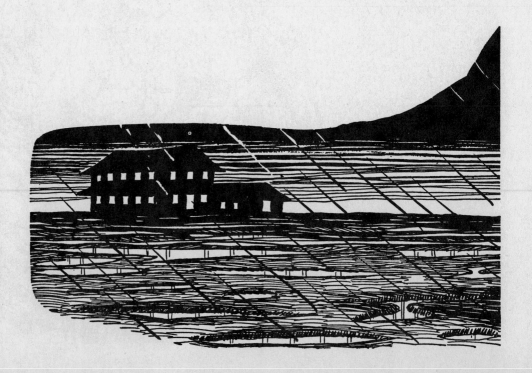

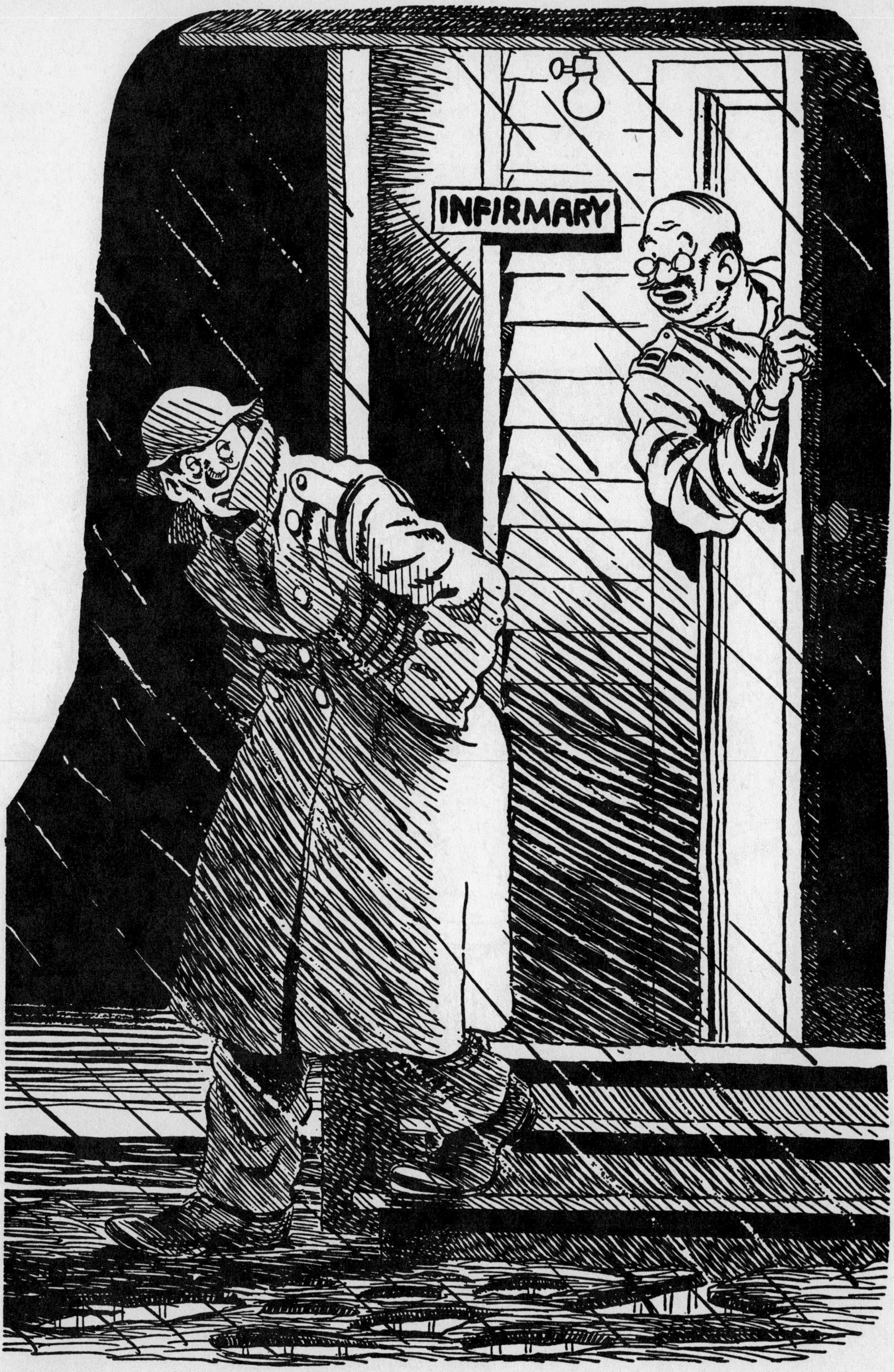
INFIRMARY

"Now, Jim—I'm going to talk to you as if you were my own son."

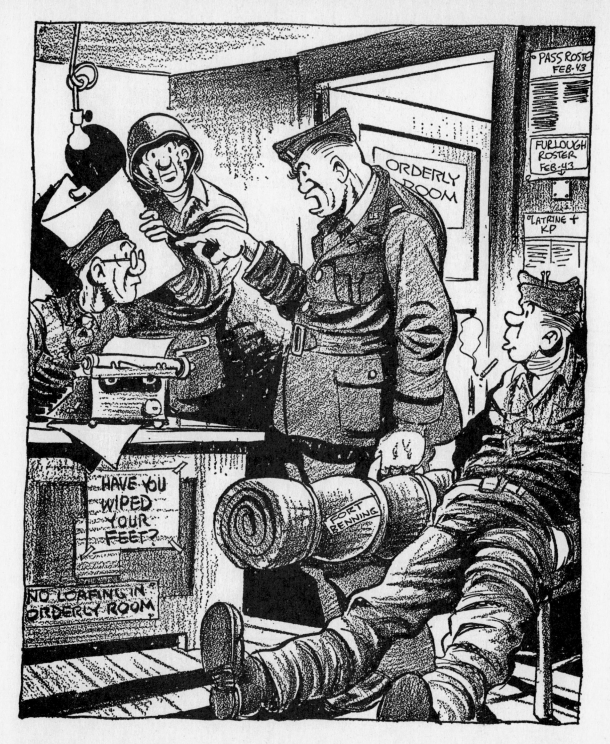

"Unnerstand, I want just as much respeck around here as if I was still first sergeant!"

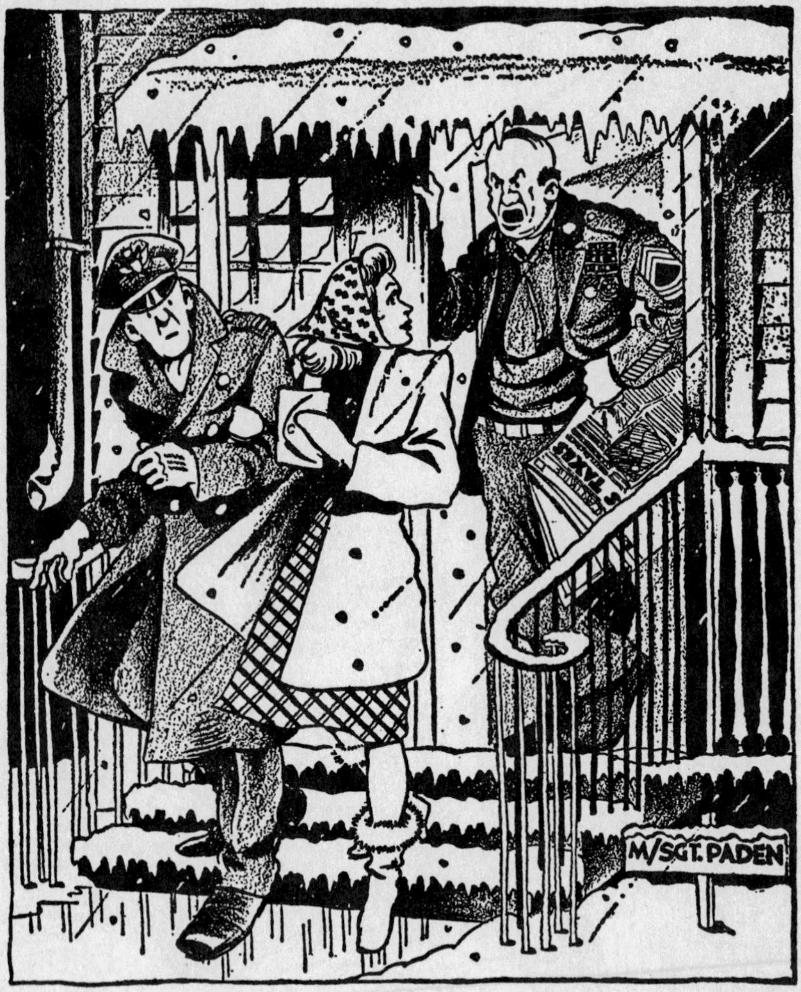
M/SGT. PADEN

". . . An' remember, if she ain't in by twelve this time, there'll be a baseball bat waitin' . . . Sir."

"That's all I have to say this morning, men. All right, dismissed. . . . I said dismissed!"

"Regimental says never mind—th' colonel got tired o' waitin' an' walked to his quarters."

"I think we shoulda been more careful with that booby-trap lecture."

*"Gimme one—wit'
mustard."*

*"Don't pay any attention to him, boys. He always acts like that when he knows it's
his fault."*

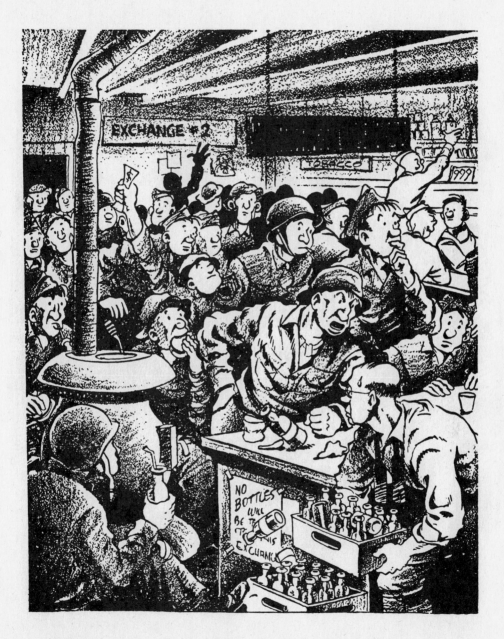

"This is fifteen minutes I been waitin'! D'ya wanna lose my business?"

"Let me take you away from all this . . ."

"Will you stop jiggling that damned hook?"

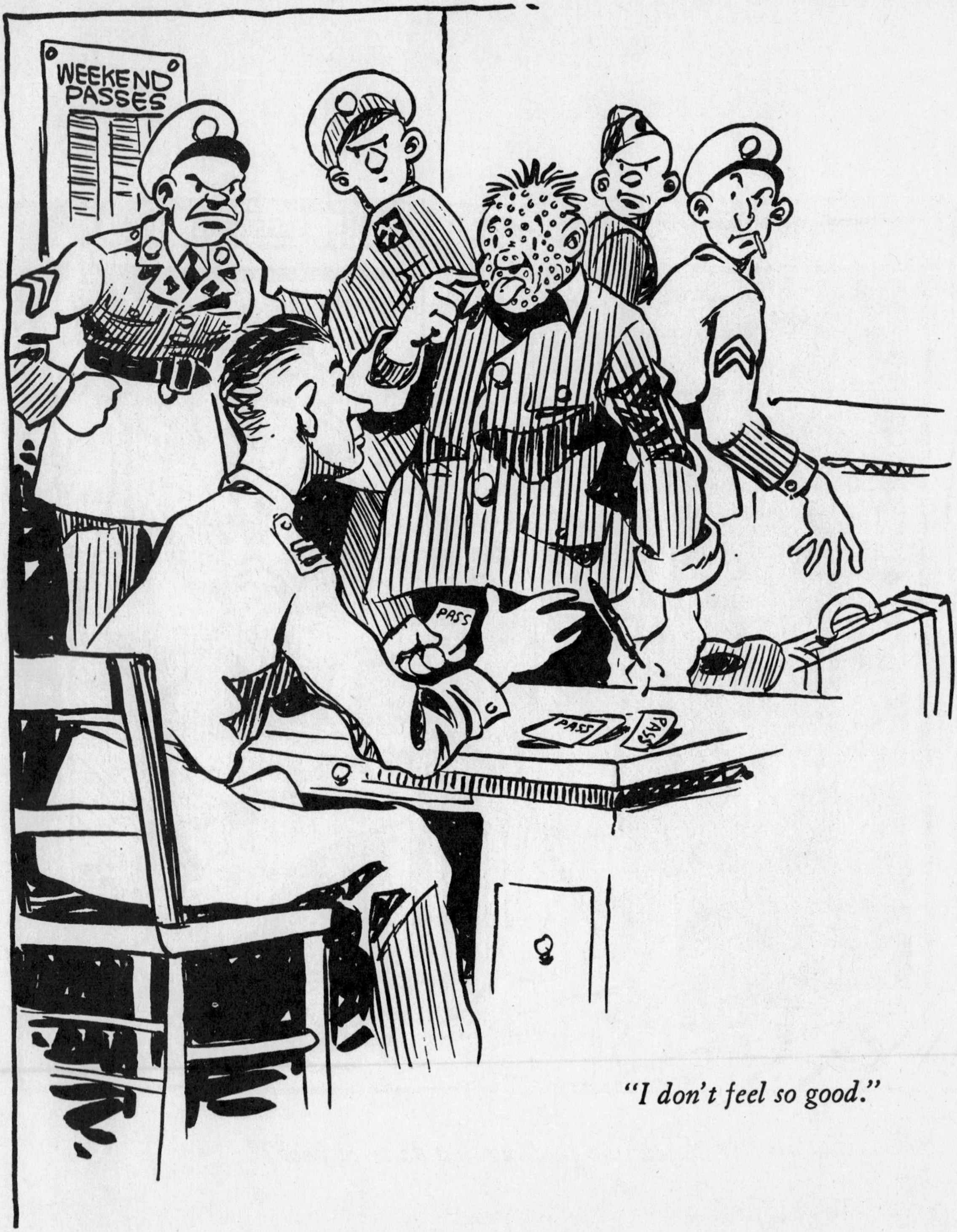
WEEKEND PASSES
PASS
PASS
PASS

"I don't feel so good."

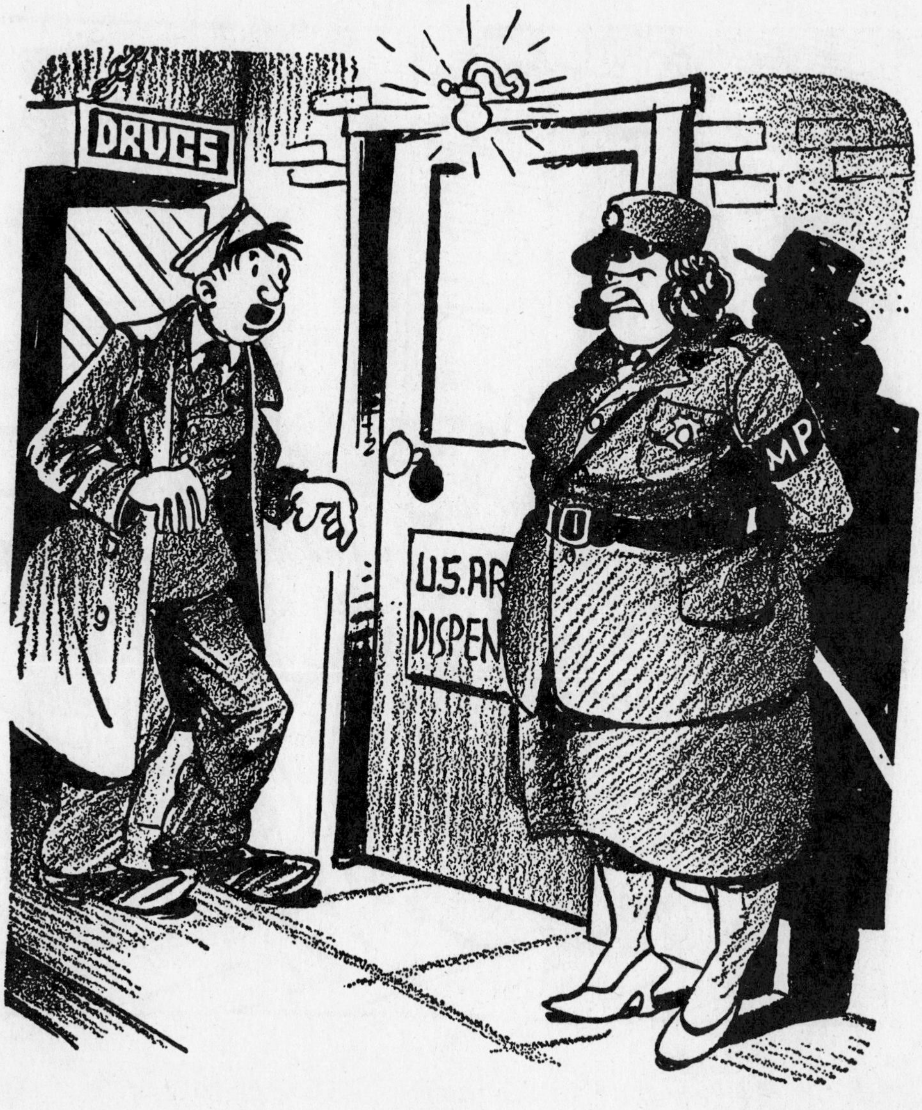
DRUGS
U.S.AR
DISPEN
MP

"Lucy!"

"*I hear the rent situation in town is pretty bad.*"

"If you're through explaining about reveille to your company commander, I'd like to report this wreck."

"Am I stripped down enough to suit ya, ma'am?"

"Don't take it so hard, friend—there will be another car before long."

"Let's make 'em all show their passes."

"Fall in fer reveille right here, boys—an' the captain sends his sympathy about th' bus situation."

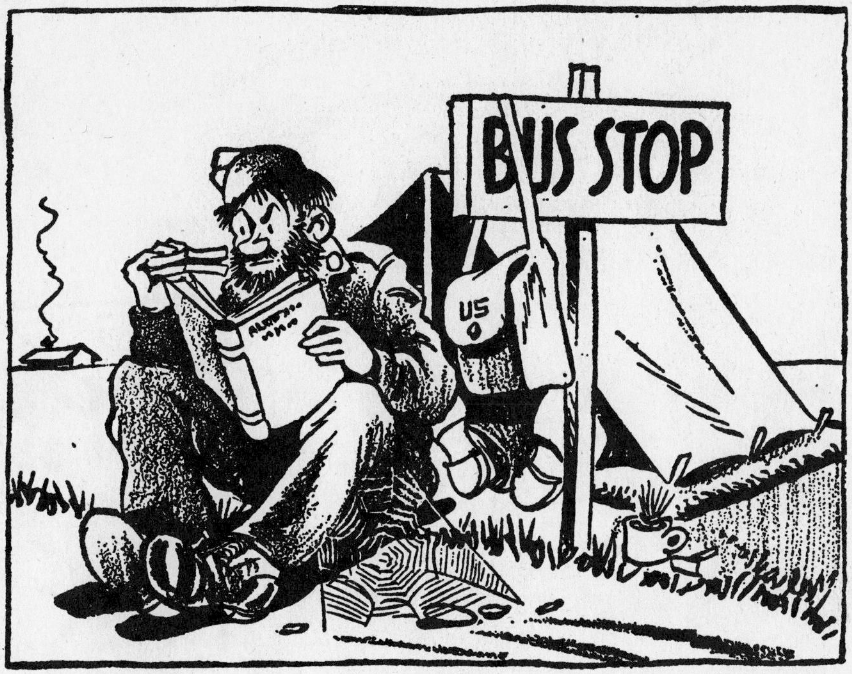
BUS STOP
US

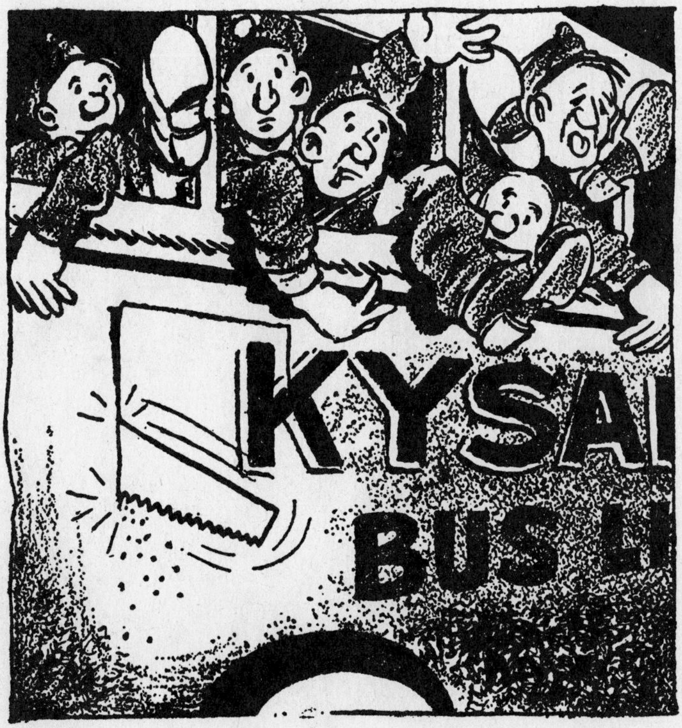
KYSA
BUS

"Now let's go over

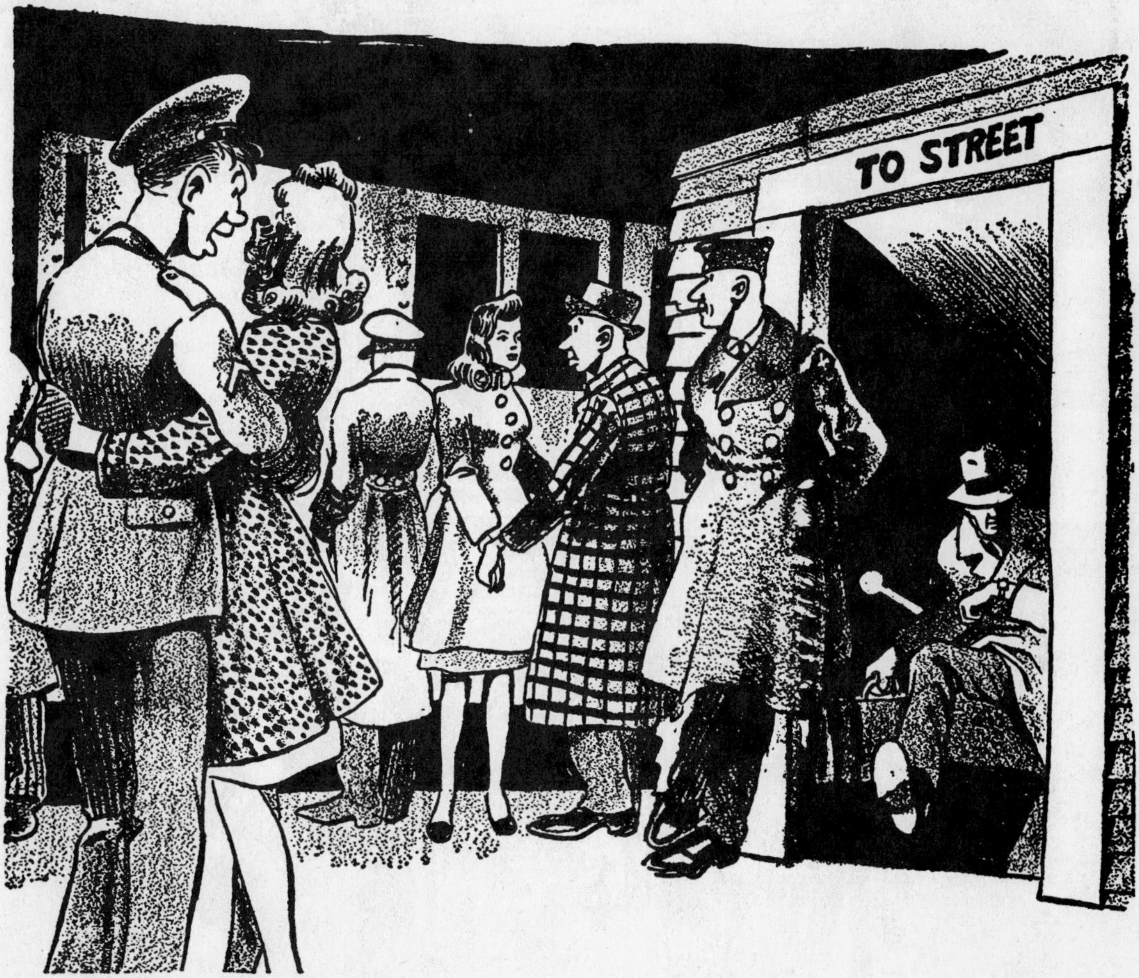
TO STREET

to the bus station."

"I've warned you before about crowding three in a seat."

"Please stay here. It adds class to my joint."

"*I have to be ready to grab the emergency brake in case anything goes wrong.*"

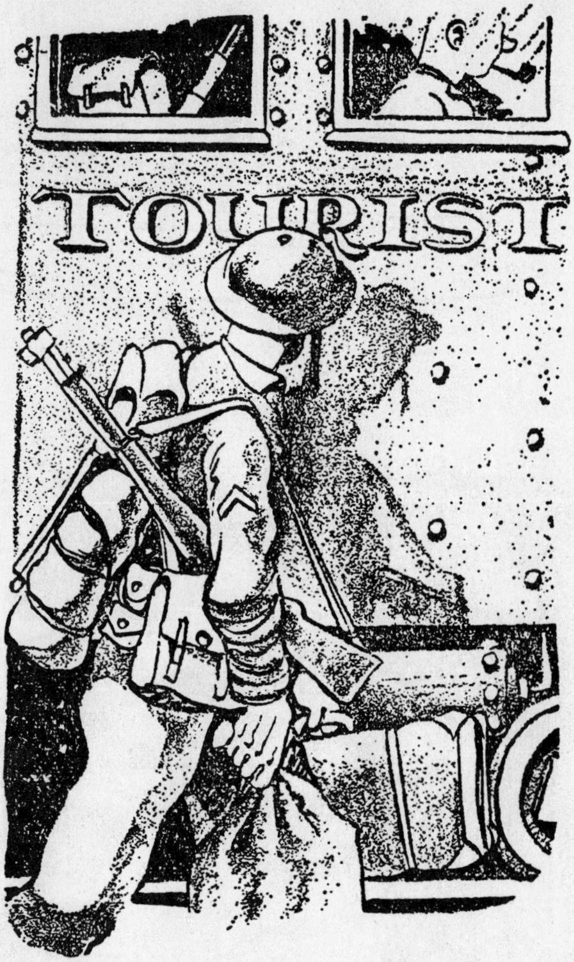
TOURIST

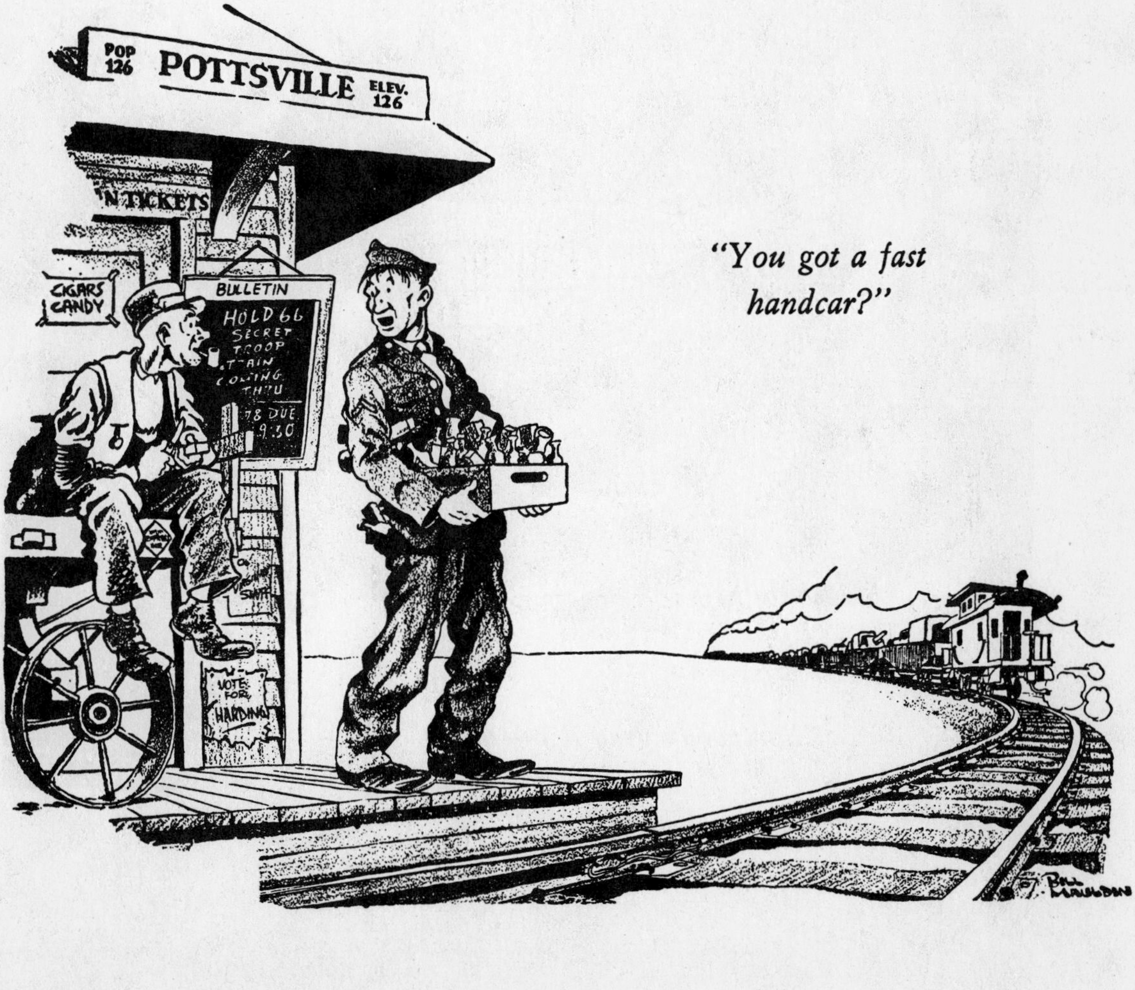
POP 126
POTTSVILLE
ELEV. 126
'N TICKETS
CIGARS CANDY
BULLETIN
HOLD 66 SECRET TROOP TRAIN COMING THRU
78 DUE 9:30
VOTE FOR HARDING

"You got a fast handcar?"

"Somebody grab her—quick!"

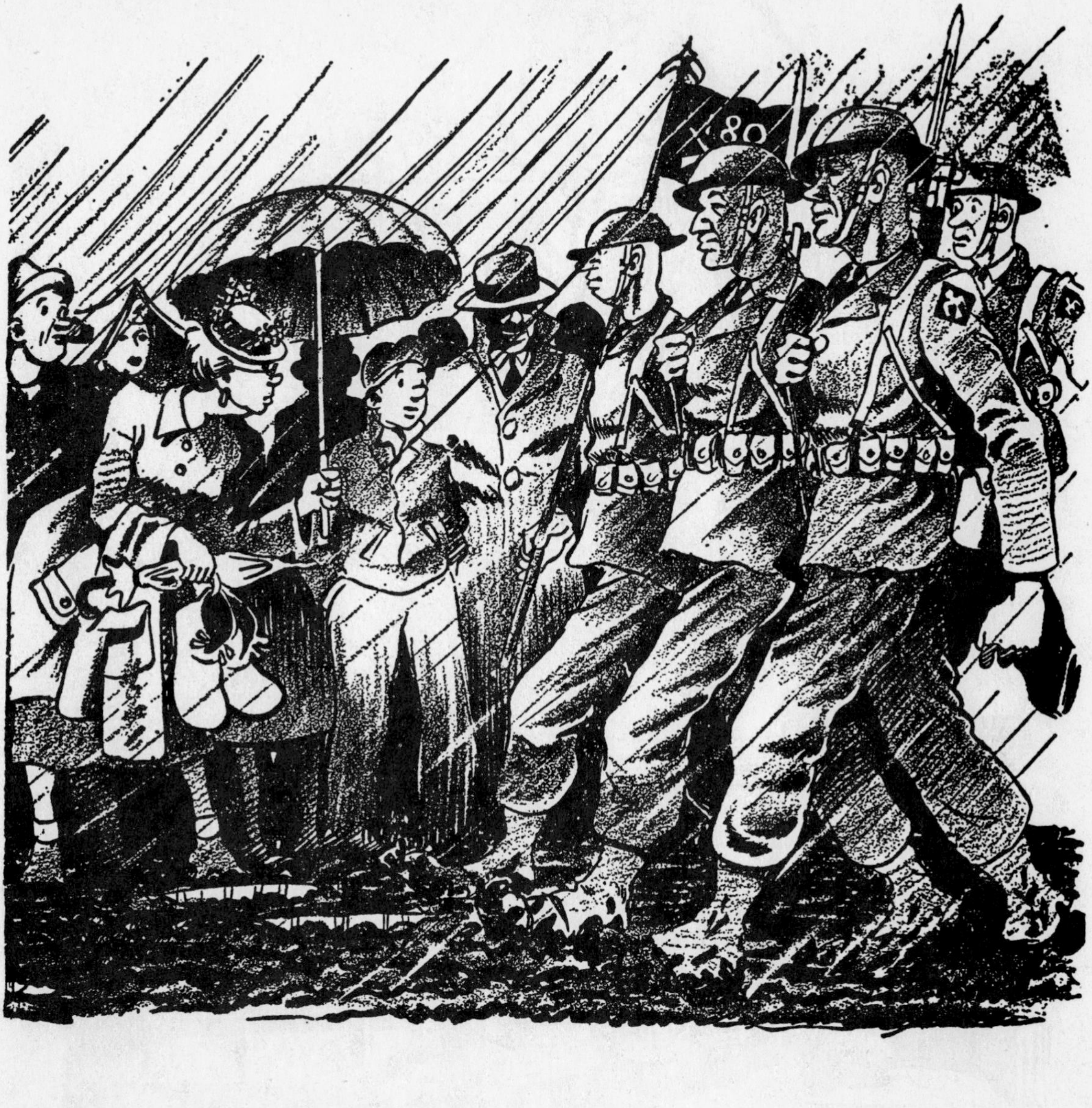
80

"I'm sorry, the War Department has ordered us not to divulge our location—oh—you say this is the War Department speaking . . ."

"I thought this wuz a awful long rest stop."

"... So this is what you call a 'rest stop.' And they only give you ten minutes every two hours? Gee, I hope I'm not boring you, asking all these questions. ..."

"Someday you guys are gonna have to learn to take no
for an answer."

"Never mind—I found one."

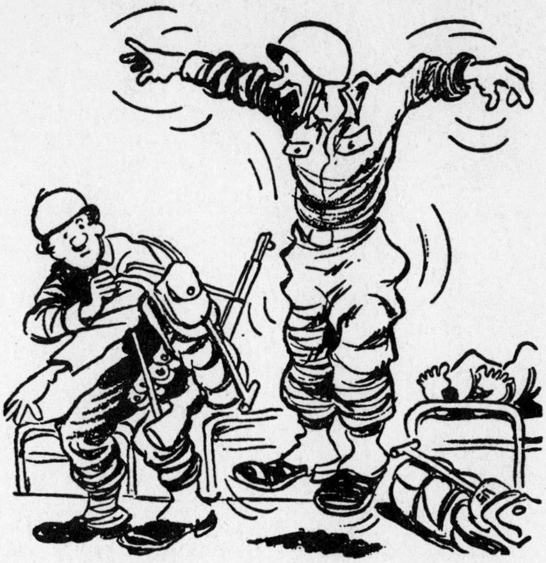

"Look—I kin fly!"

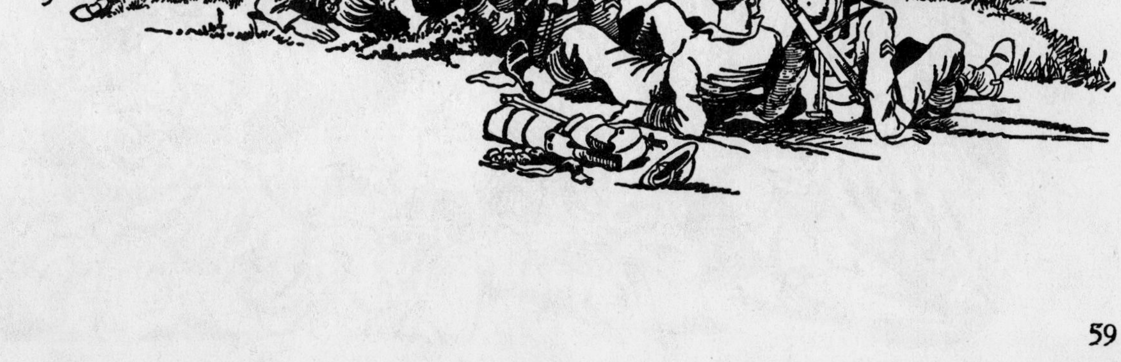
"I'D WALK A MILE FOR A CAMEL!"

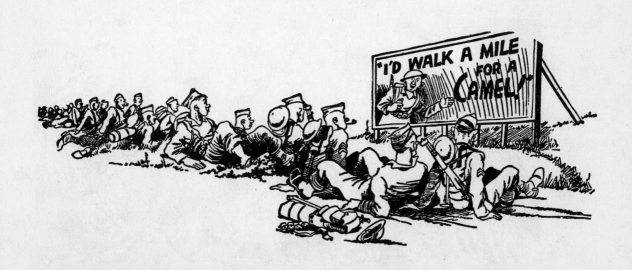

"Must be cheap gas. I wuz gettin' used to high octane."

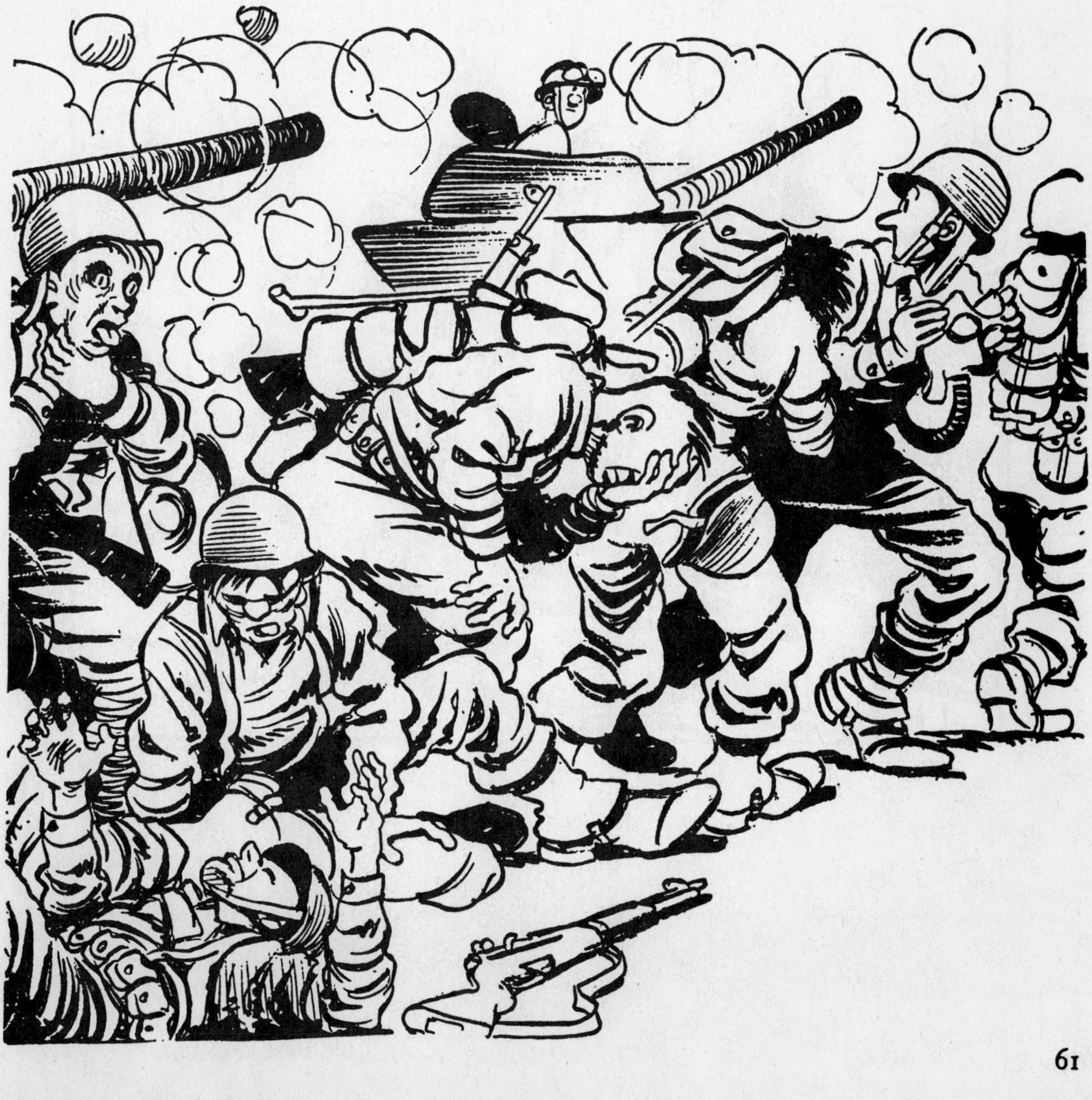

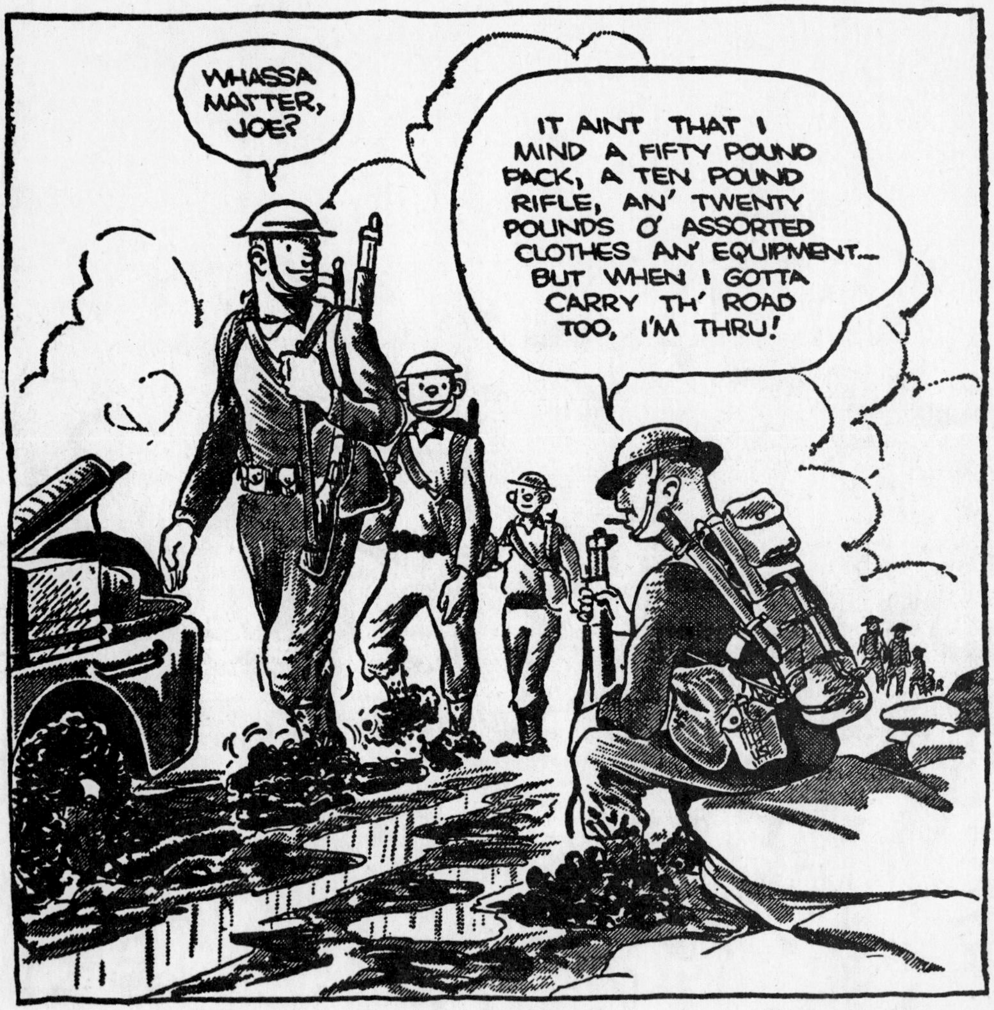
WHASSA MATTER, JOE?
IT AINT THAT I MIND A FIFTY POUND PACK, A TEN POUND RIFLE, AN' TWENTY POUNDS O' ASSORTED CLOTHES AN' EQUIPMENT... BUT WHEN I GOTTA CARRY TH' ROAD TOO, I'M THRU!

"Go tell yer old man if he wants this topsoil back to come git it."

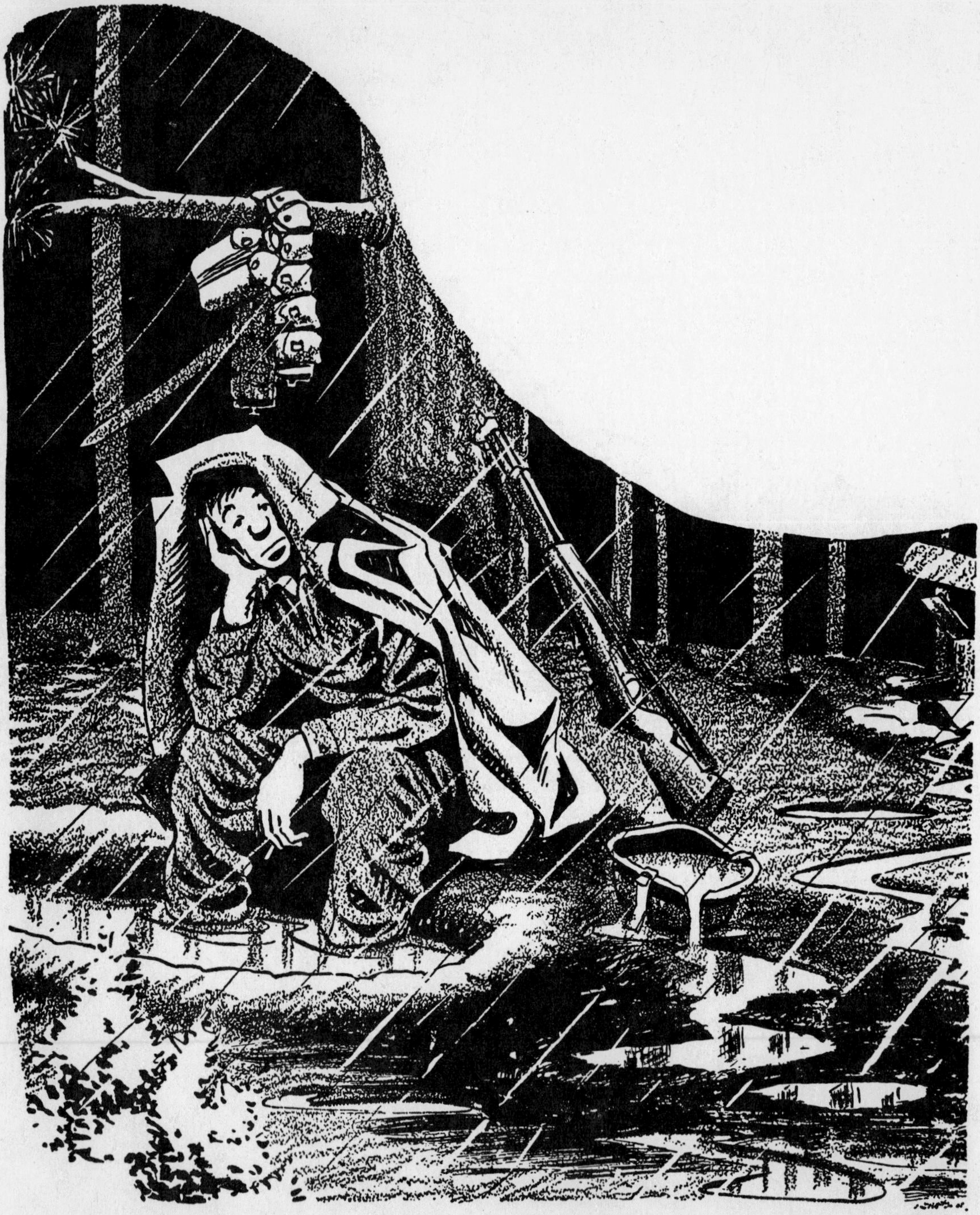

"Coffee does me like that, too. I can't sleep a wink."

66 *"Dang it, ya promised me a week's K.P. if I missed reveille again."*

"I don't want to have to warn you men again about building these confounded fires."

The last match

"I wuz just kiddin', Joe—you got three letters."

"Corp'l Ginnis an' his Very pistol will now contribute
th' Star o' Bethlehem."

"Ain't you never seen a man in a fox-hole before?"

"Buck up, men—we'll have th' wind behind us on th' way back."

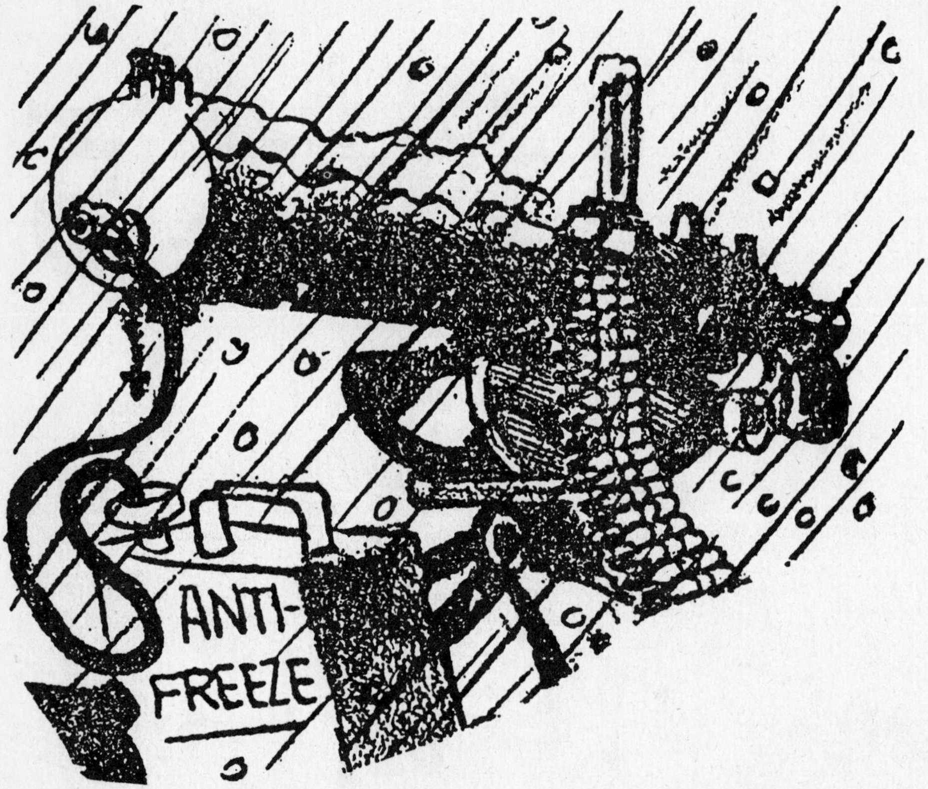
ANTI-
FREEZE

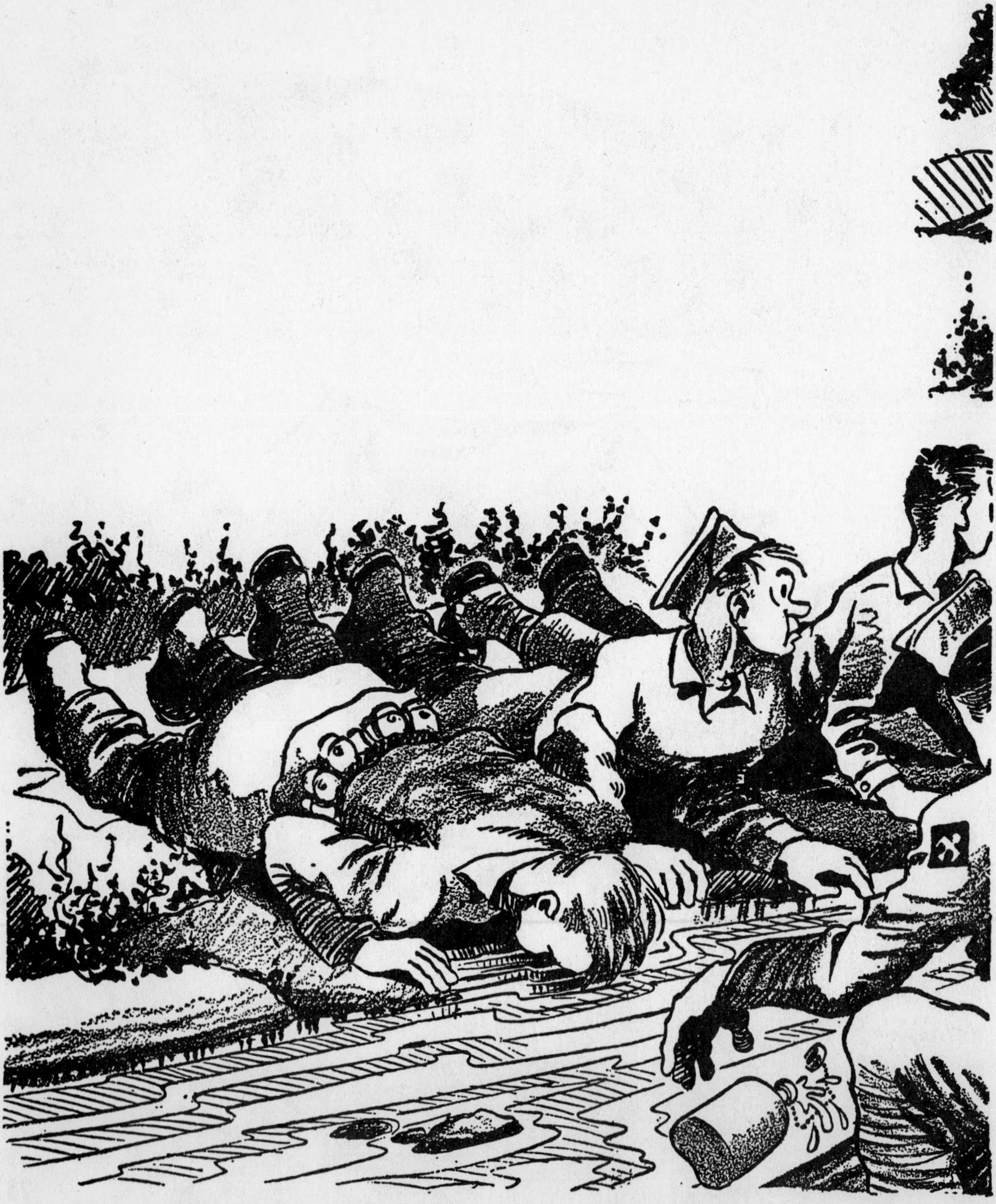

"Anybody got some more soap?"

"You left a ring around the edge."

"Go back, buddy—it ain't worth it."

"You know *we always fall out with clean khaki an' ties for Sunday dinner!*"

"Ceiling zero. Visibility zero. Range 200 yards."

"I got tired o' tellin' you all."

"If ya won't learn, at least put this where it'll do th' most good."

"Now they want we should paint a white stripe down the middle."

"Relax—it's only a maneuver."

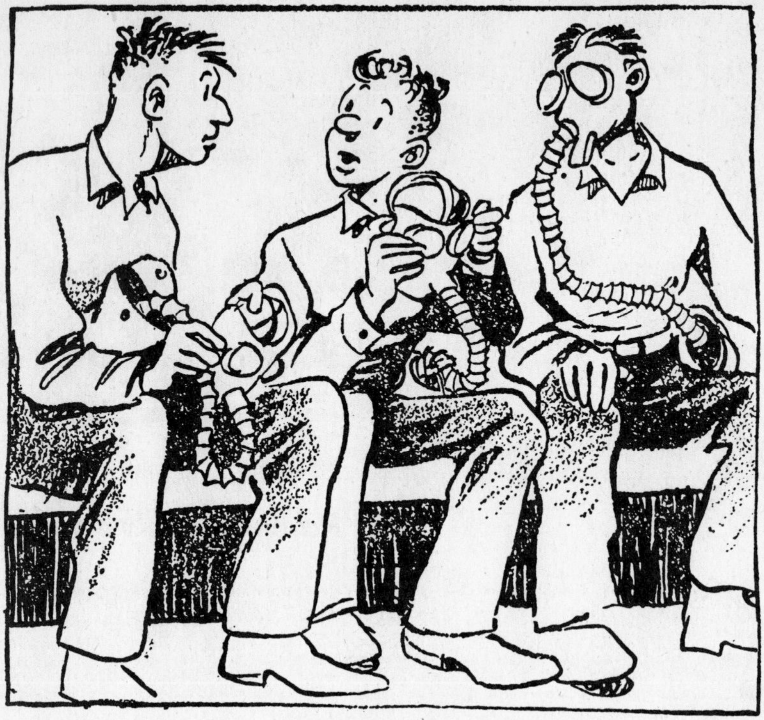

"I got halitosis."

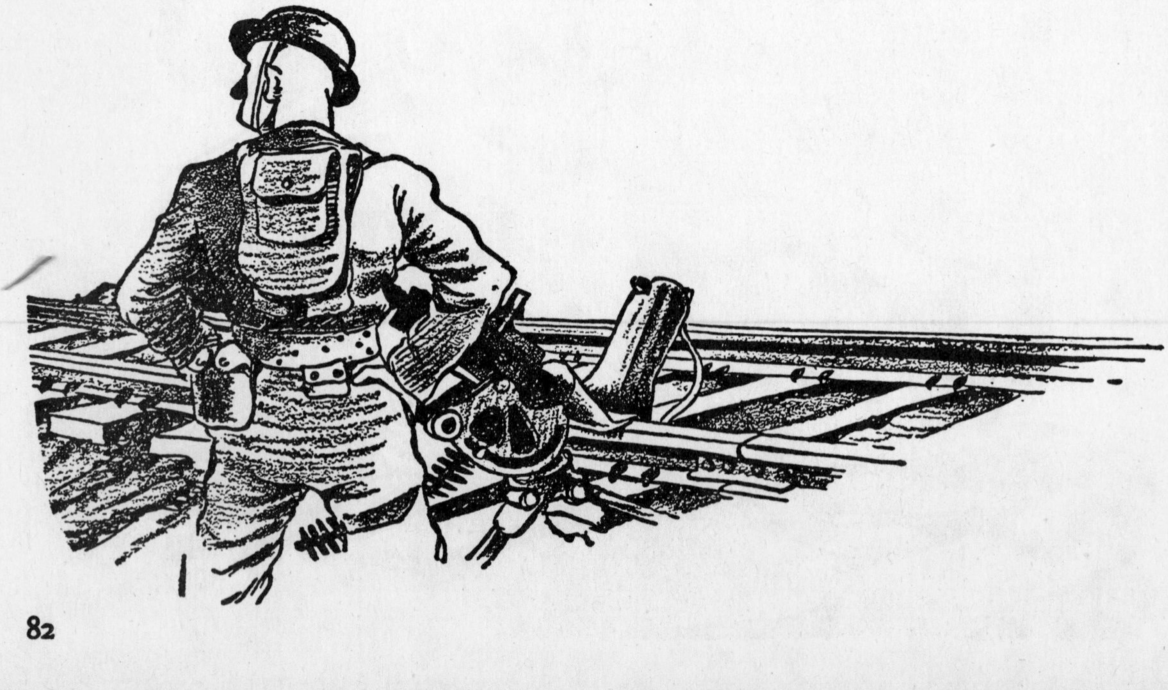

"But I want to use the net. It gives my men confidence."

"O.K.—it's a swap, if ya throw in yer tin hat."

"George Fielding Eliot is right. Firepower should be sackerficed for mobility."

"Touche!"

"Nice work, Mac! I heard a muffled scream as he went by."

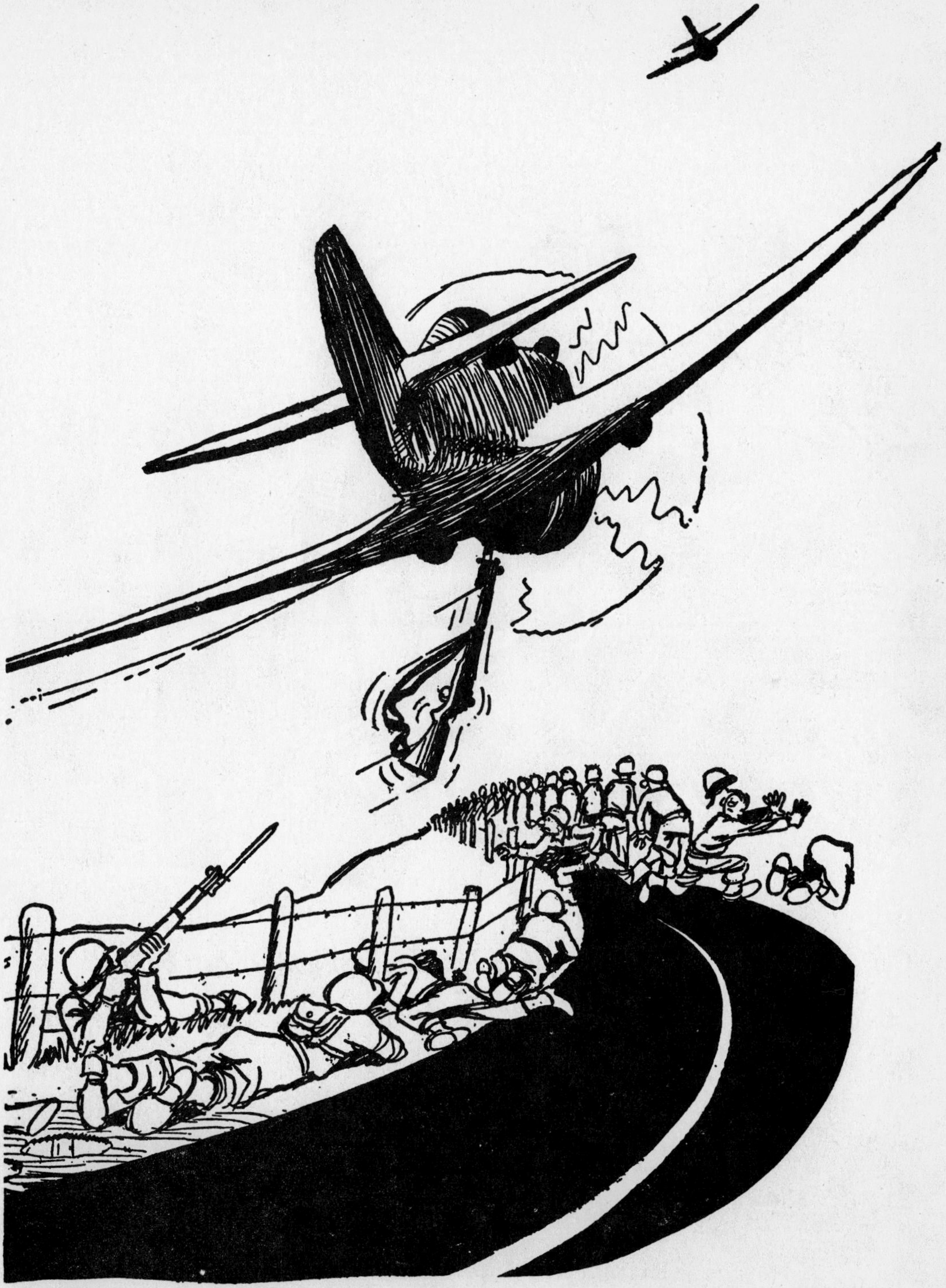

"Get some spirit inta it! Th' guy's a Jap! He just got yer best buddy!
Now he's comin' at ya!"

"I gotta hand it to ya. I didn't think that buried treasure rumor would work."

"Here comes Hagood to butt in on th' conversation."

Louisiana maneuver umpire shot by wax pellet from blank cartridge. Culprits say they resented decision ordering them back twenty yards to new positions in rocky ground. Officer's condition reported painful but not critical. (News item)

"*We bagged fourteen Blues this way yestiddy.*"

"*Awright, Mike—you been wantin' to drive awhile.*"

"I hate to bother ya at a time like this, but has anybody seen
a pair o' shoes layin' around?"

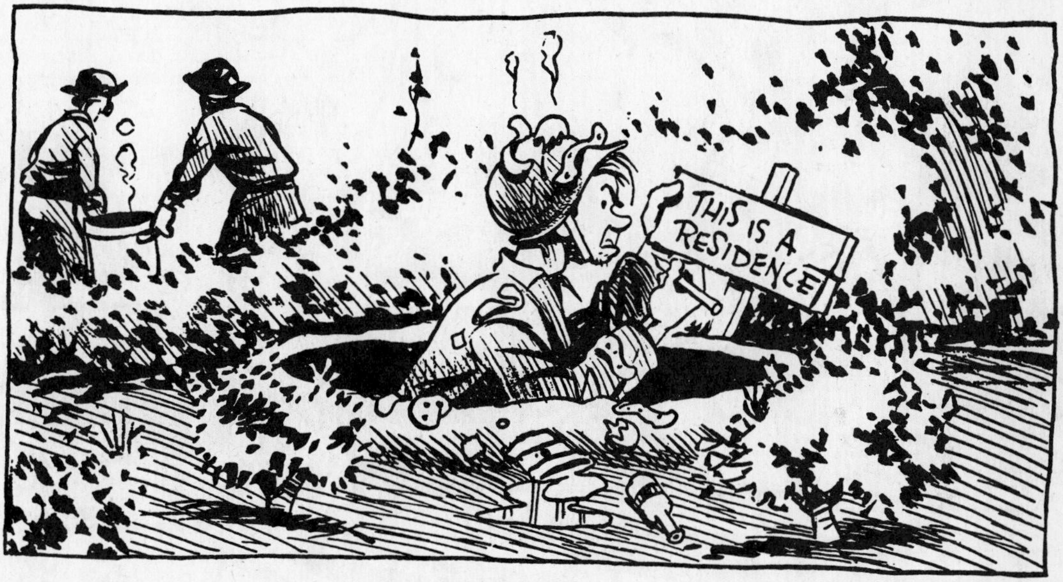
THIS IS A RESIDENCE

"Don't ask foolish questions. Th' schedule calls fer calisthenics. We'll start with th' left eyelid."

Overseas

It's a long jump from garrison cartoons to war cartoons. The next few pages, mostly about Sicily, might be called transitional—sort of maneuver jokes, with live ammunition.

The rest of the war drawings, about Italy, France, and Germany, are grouped, as in the first part of this book, by subject matter rather than sequence. For instance, a 1943 cartoon about freezing in the mountains of Southern Italy might appear with one drawn two years later about slush in Germany, on the grounds that while the style of the pictures may differ, the soldiers *in* the pictures felt pretty much the same about the weather.

The last group in the book, about the end of the war and going home, are in the order they were drawn.

"Yessir, I got my Purple Heart—nossir, I ain't married—yessir, my blood is type 'A'—if I got any left after all these questions."

"You're not on the job, sentry—a sniper almost got me."

"That's no general—you got the chief of police."

"Dang clever booby trap! I kinda hate to disturb 'em . . ."

"You're right. Th' town has been occupied three days . . ."

"I told *ya* this damn building *wuz* a menace. If it ain't tore down by
mornin' I'll have ya arrested!"

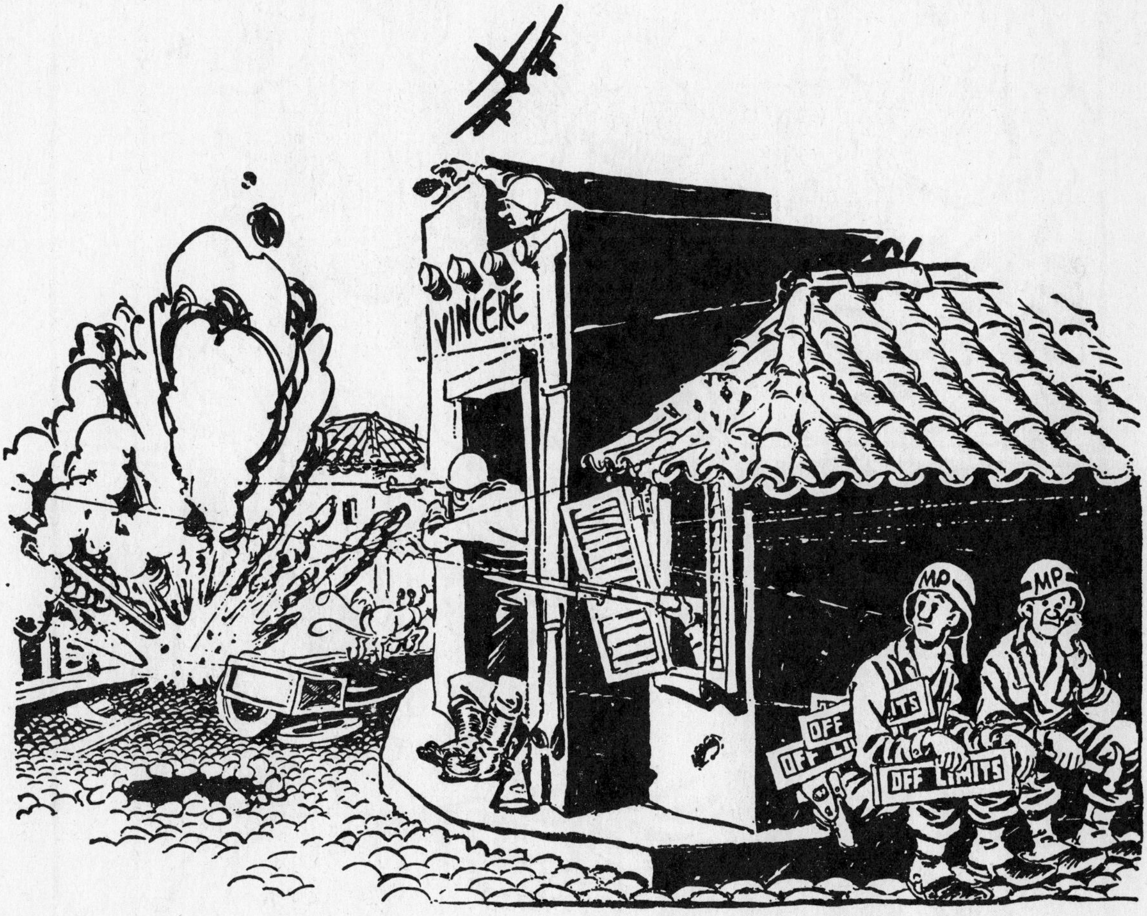
VINCERE
MP
MP
OFF LIMITS
OFF LIMITS
OFF LIMITS
OFF LIMITS

"*Sometimes I think Carmen ain't as innocent as she looks. She says she wants to 'emigrate.'*"

"*What say we go down an' strafe 'em?*"

"*No, thank you. My mother says I'm too young to smoke.*"

"Hurry up with that towel. You ain't th' only one wot's got soap in his eyes!"

"Anybody wanna trade a cocoa fer two lemonades?"

"Oh—I beg yer pardon—I didn't know I wuz breakin' convoy."

"Well, if it ain't 'Slinky' Costello, 'Knife' Randuzzi, an' 'Baby-Face' Stampione!
Remember me, boys? I'm that thick-headed flatfoot from Precinct Seven . . ."

*"Stop shootin' at him, ya idiot! Wanna give
away our position?"*

"You hear that, Fernando? Italy surrendered! You ain't a enemy no more!"

"I'd ruther cover th' gun. I won't hafta dry myself with a oily rag."

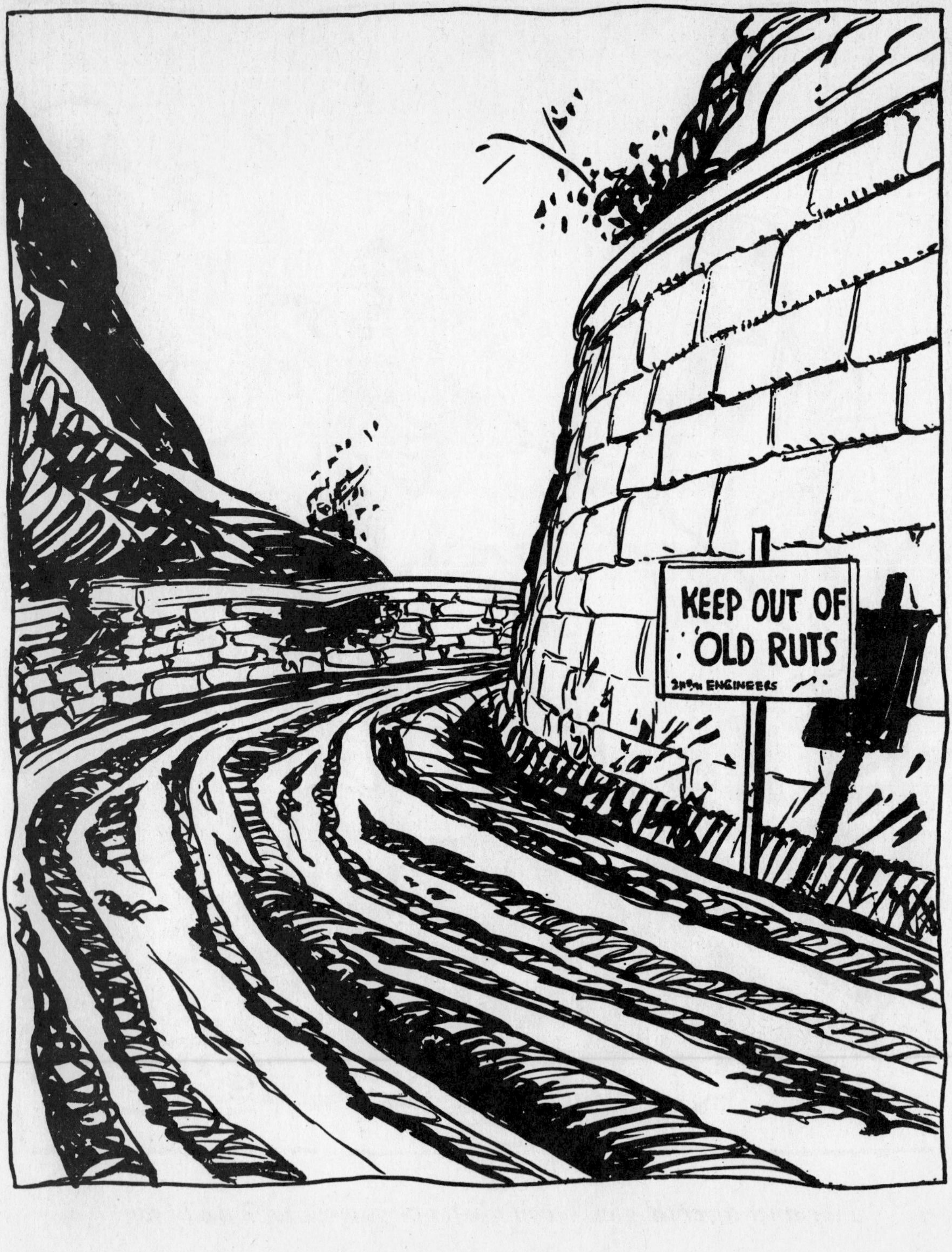
KEEP OUT OF
OLD RUTS

"Now that ya mention it, it does sound like th' patter of rain on a tin roof."

"Th' socks ain't dry yet, but we kin take in th' cigarettes."

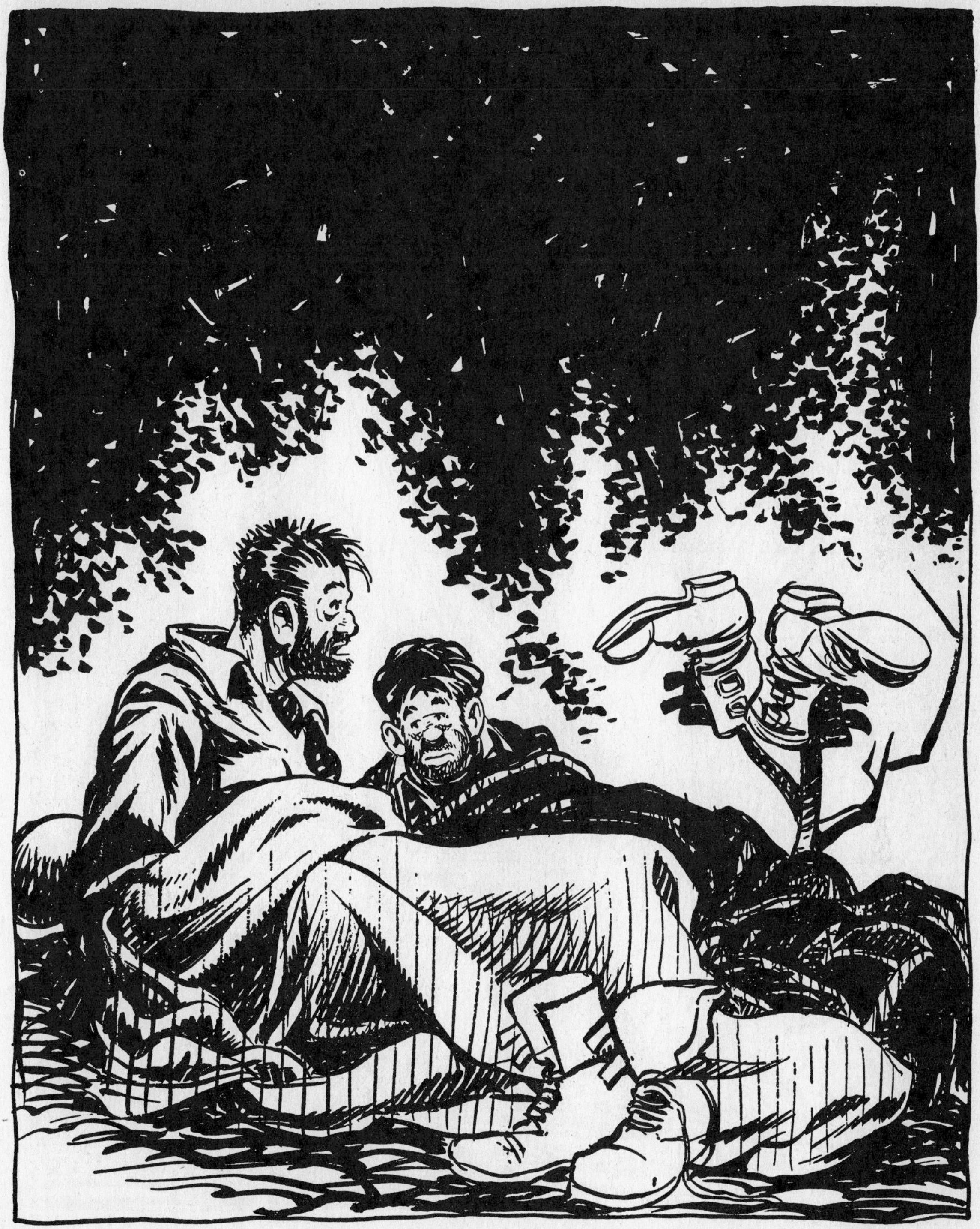

"Expectin' rain?"

"*Let 'im in. I wanna see a critter I kin feel sorry fer.*"

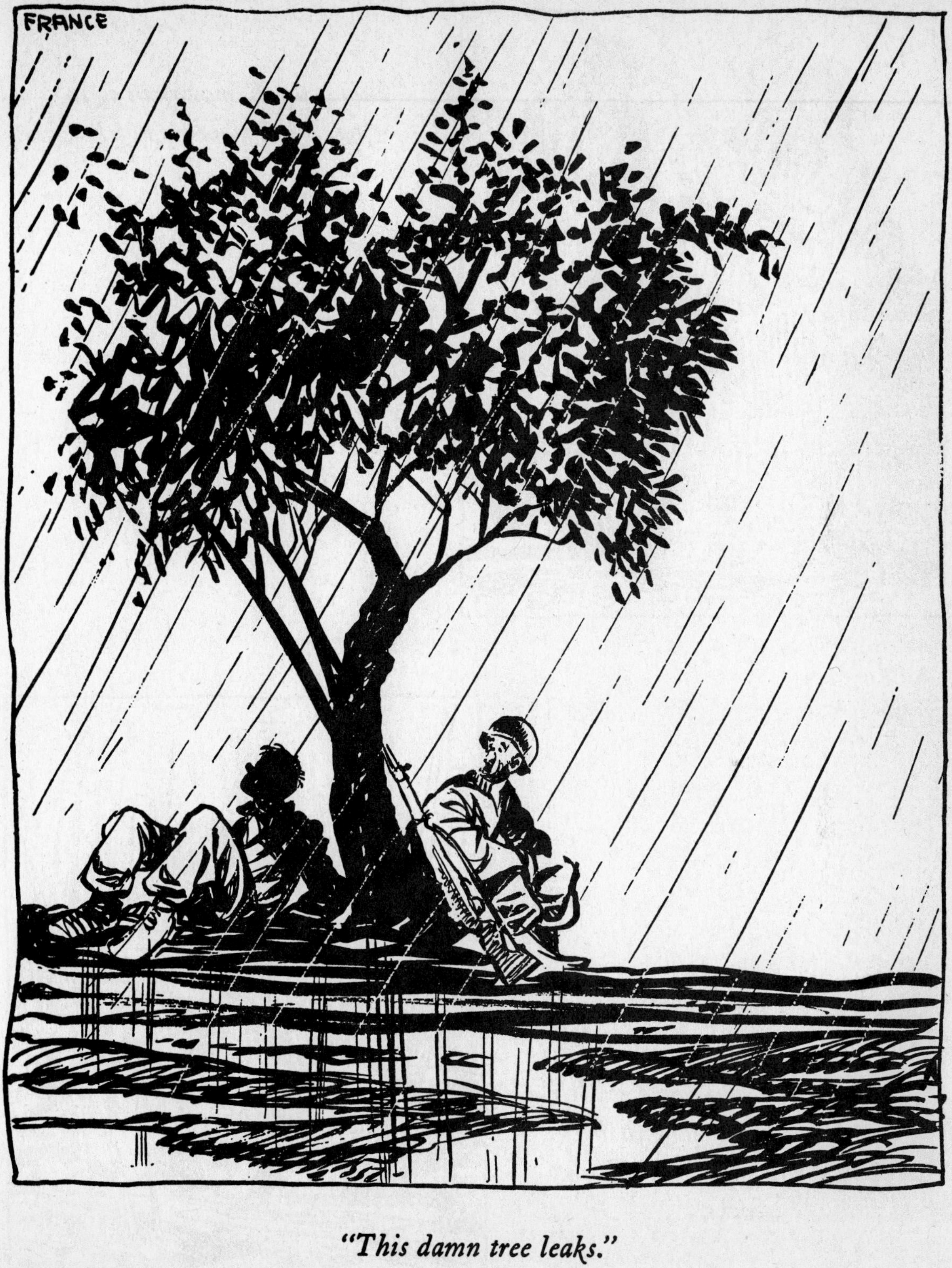
FRANCE

"This damn tree leaks."

"Run it up th' mountain ag'in, Joe. It ain't hot enough."

"Joe, yestiddy ya saved my life an' I swore I'd pay ya back. Here's my last pair o' dry socks."

"Fire two more fer effect. I'm makin' a stovepipe."

"I just ain't worth a damn in th' morning without a hot cup o' coffee."

"Ya usin' two blankets or three?"

"Remember that warm, soft mud last summer?"

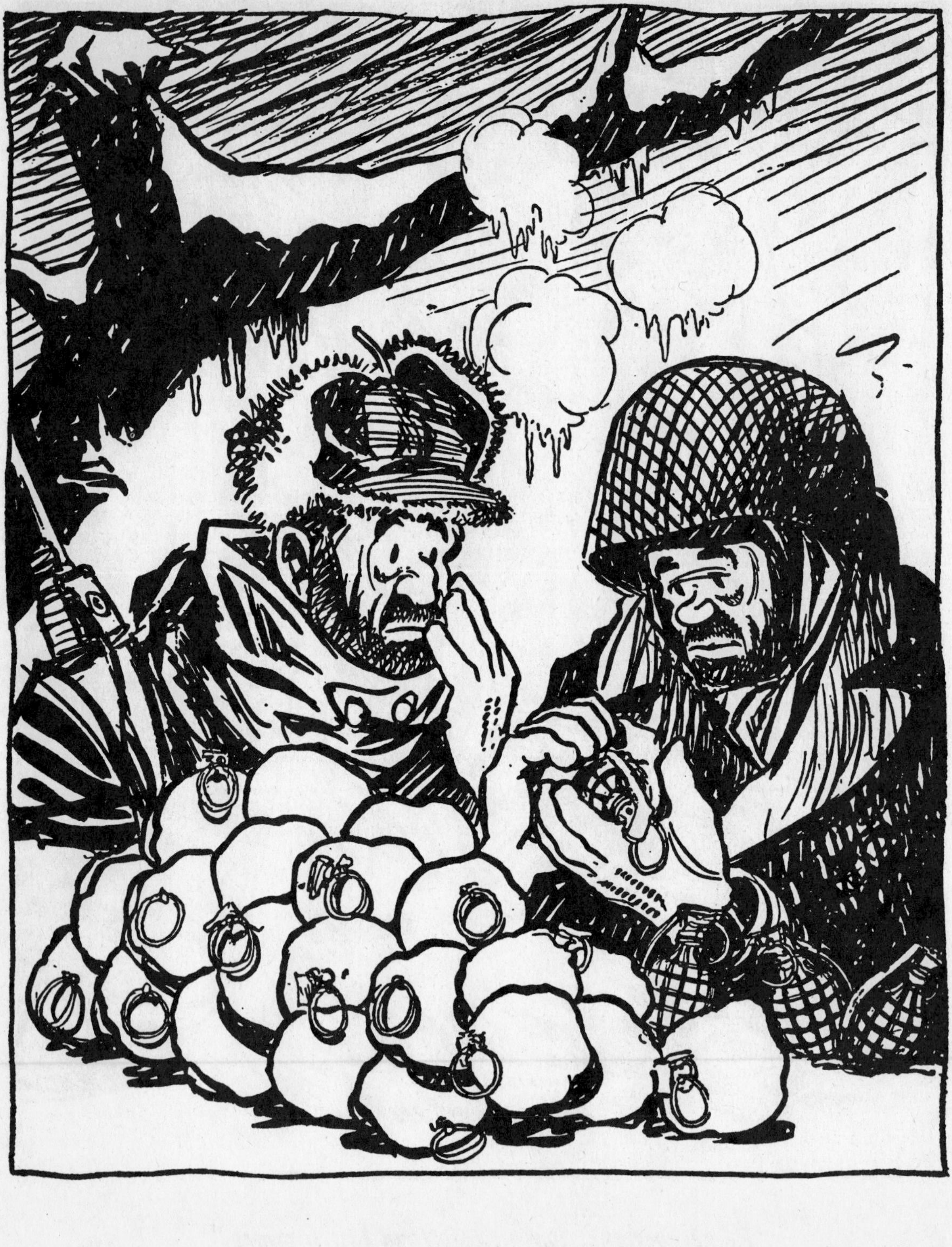

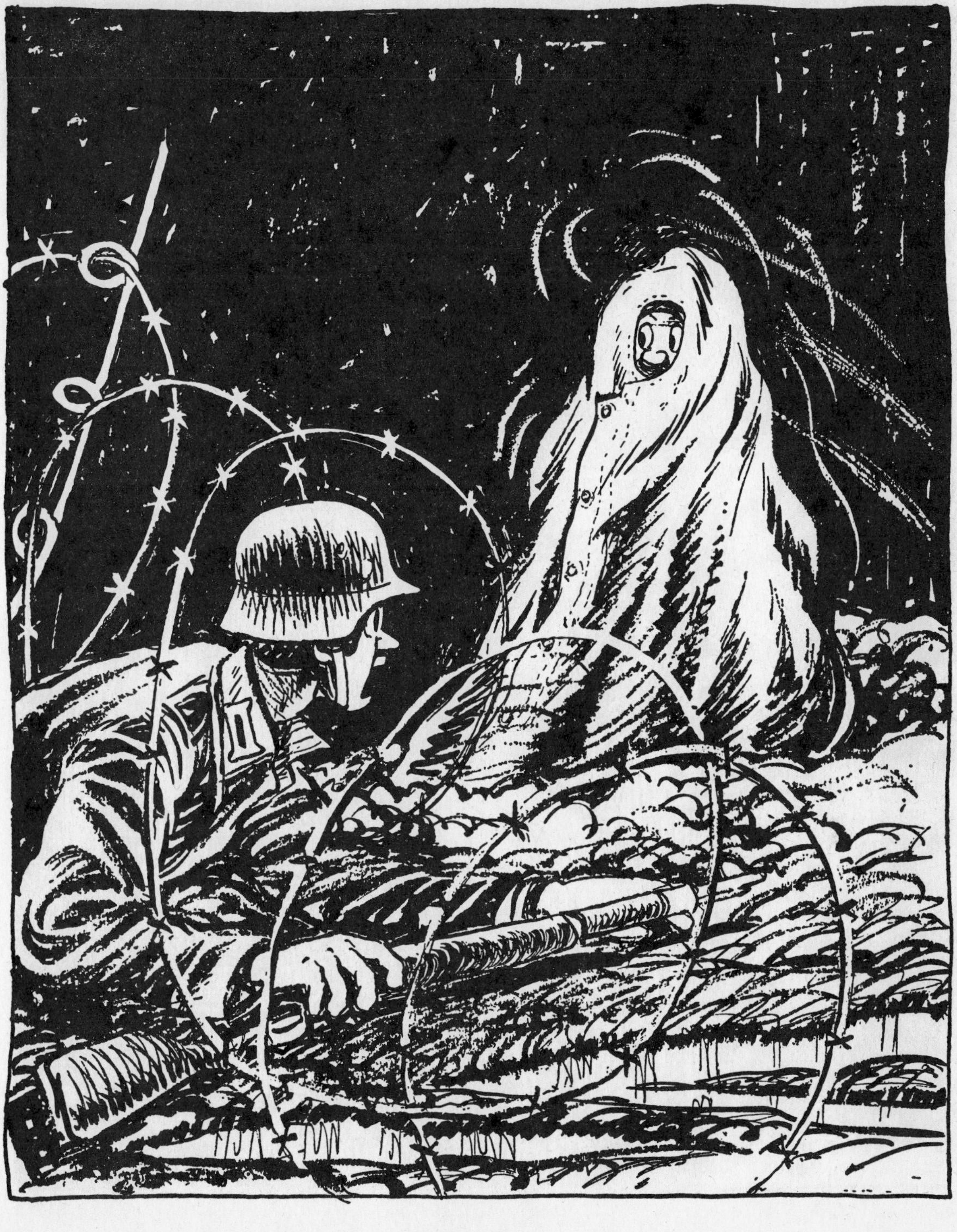

"Mein Gott!"

"A experienced field sojer will figger out a way to sleep warm an' dry. Let me know when ya do."

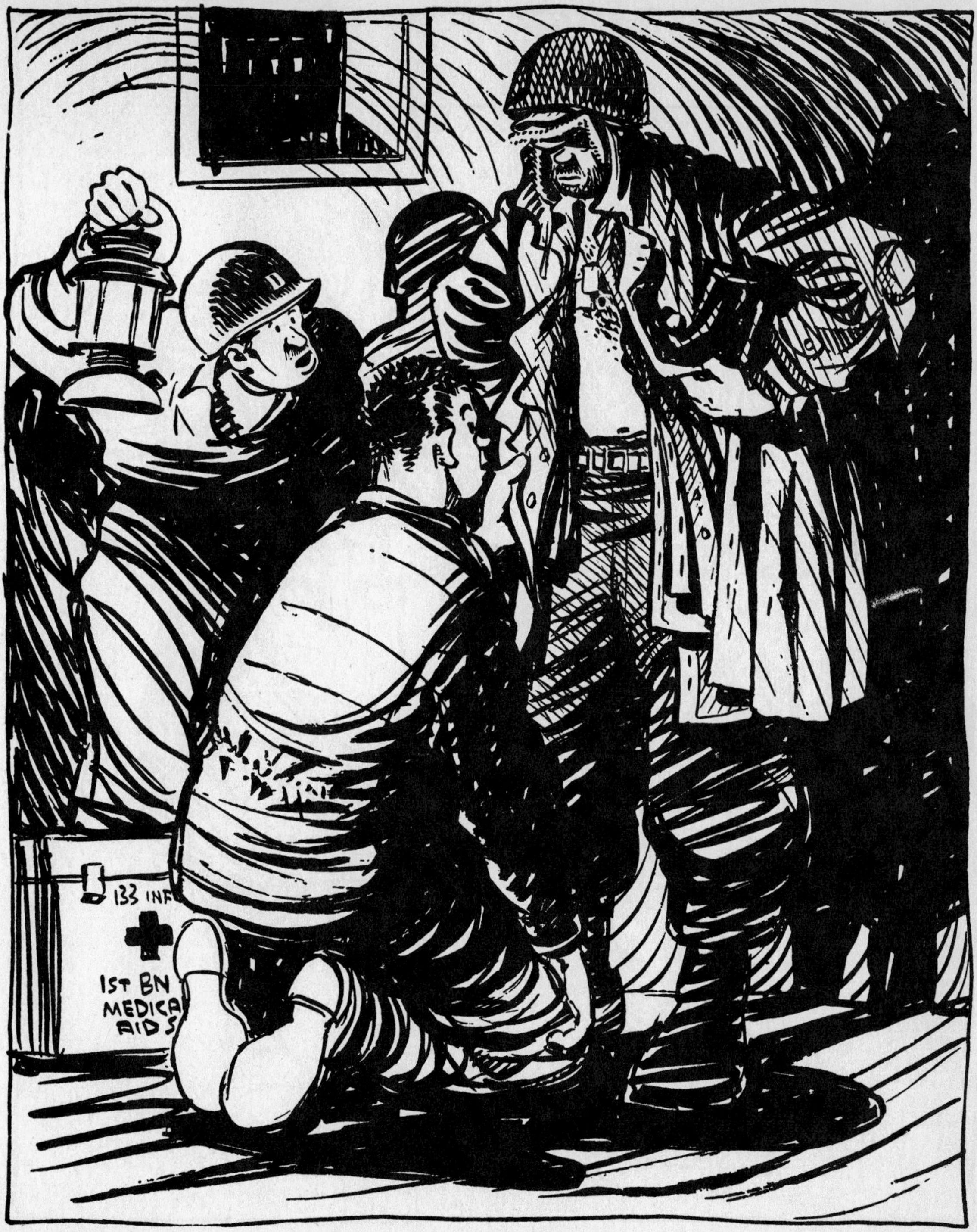
133 INF
1ST BN
MEDICA
AIDS

"Heat rash."

"Yer dern tootin' my sniffles is serious. I been drawin' mortar fire."

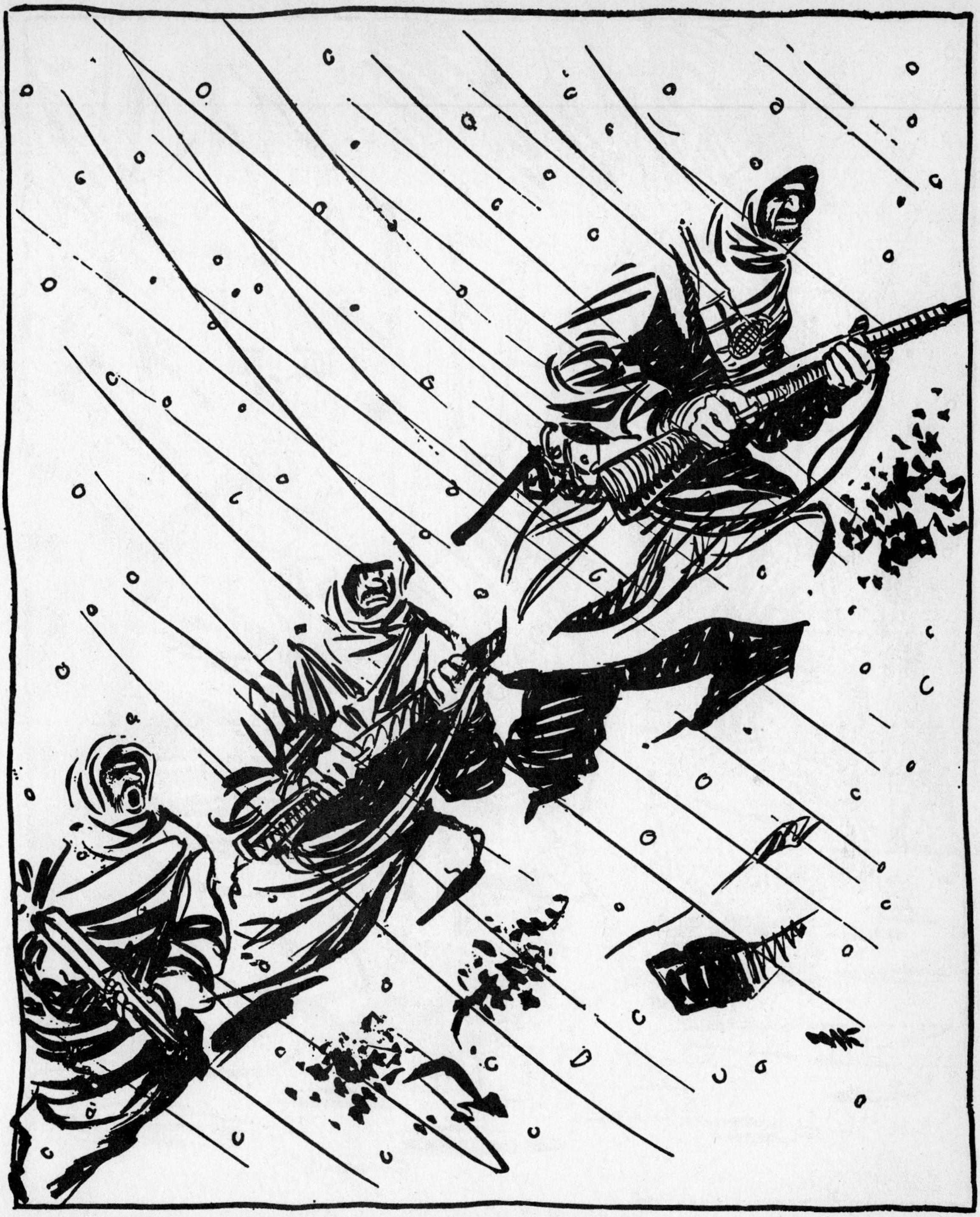

"*Mush!*"

"Them's my unmentionables."

"*Them infantry guys is chucklin' like fiends. We blew up a supply train haulin' over-coats an' blankets to th' krauts.*"

129

"Sergeant, go requisition that fire."

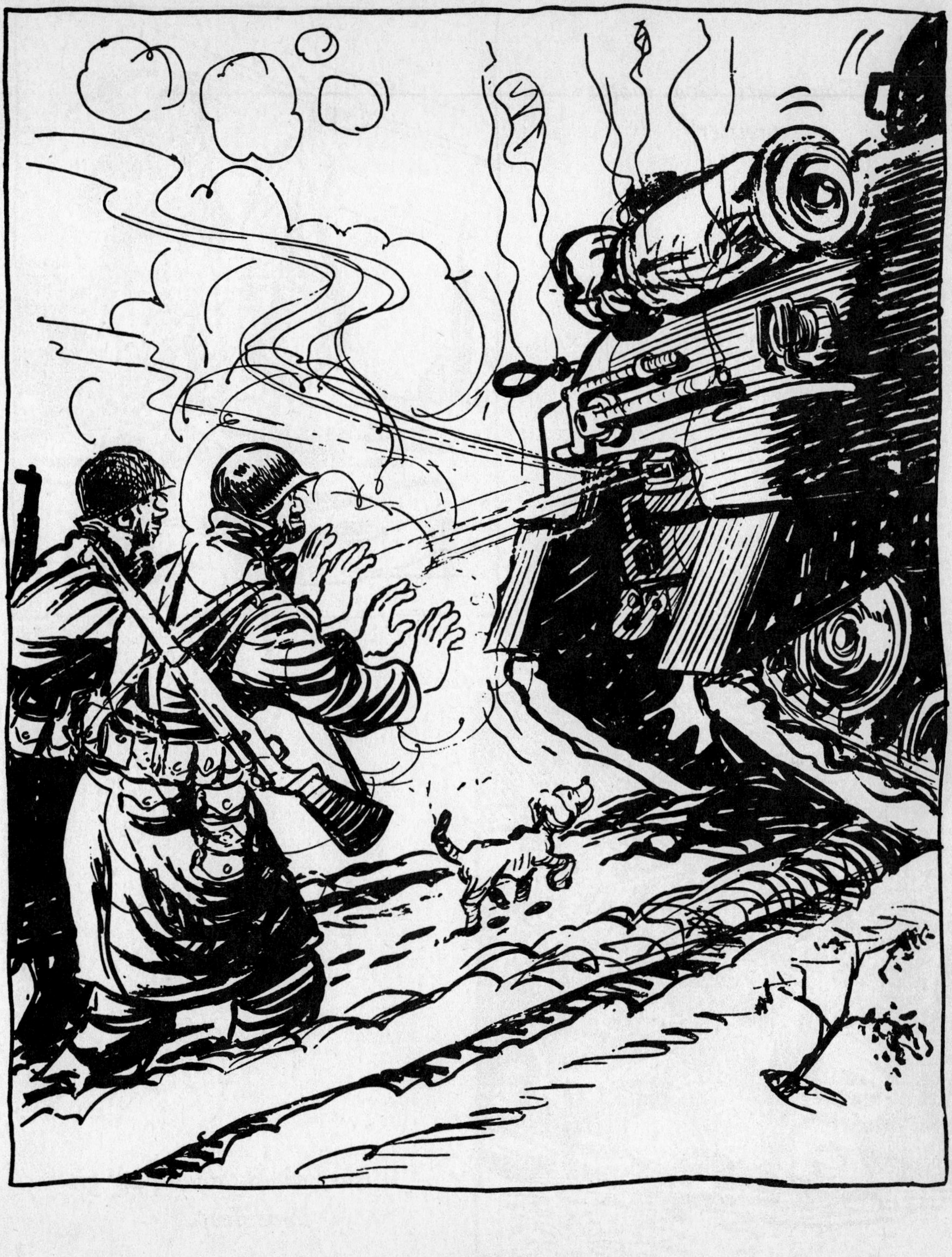

"Footprints. God, wotta monster!"

"Wisht I could stand up an' git some sleep."

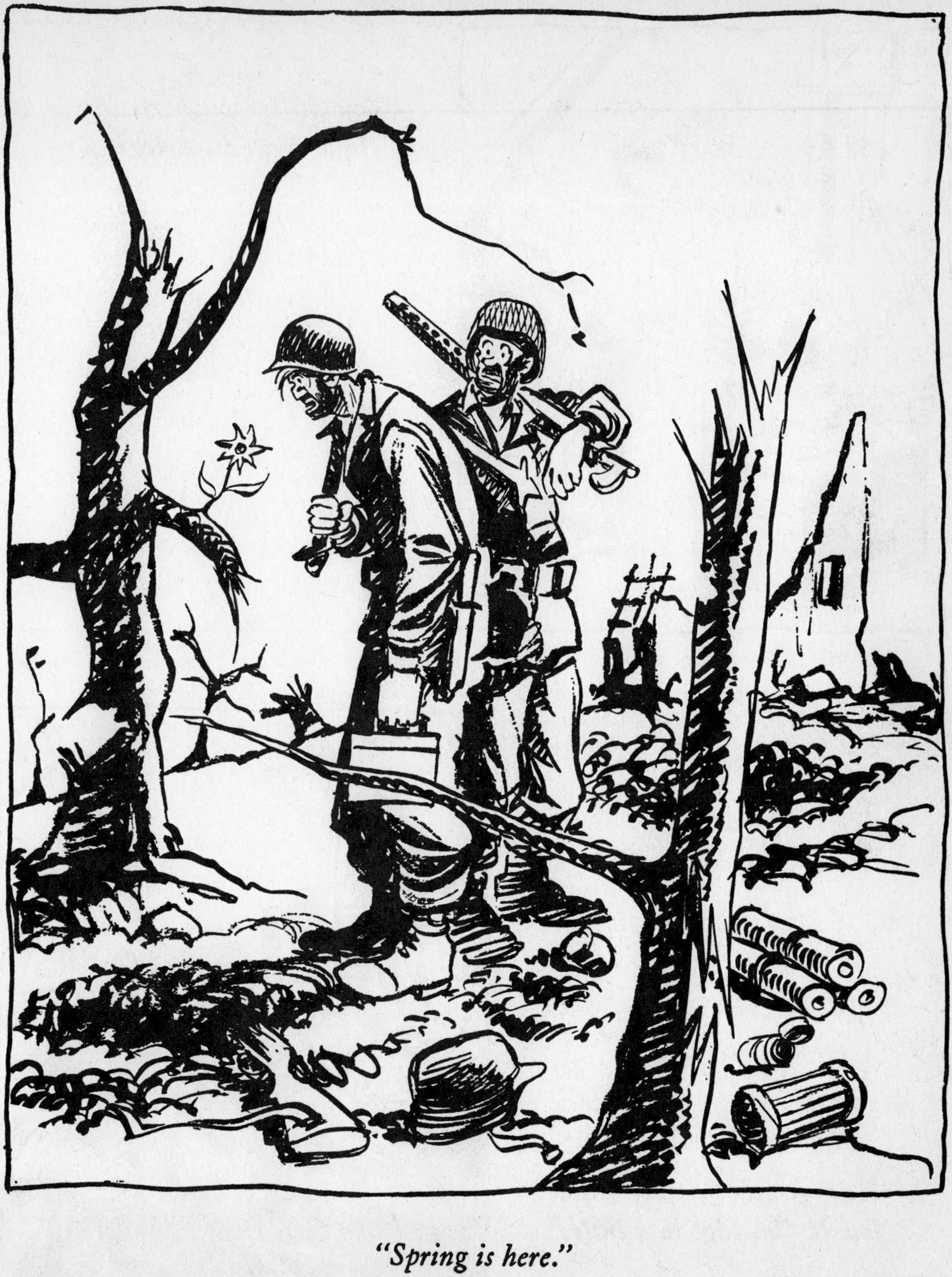

"Spring is here."

"You fellers oughta carry a little dirt t'dig holes in."

"He's gittin' th' fever, Joe. Now let 'im edge in a little."

"Hope it ain't a rocky beach. Me feet's tender since they got webbed."

135

"When ya hit th' water swish yer feet around. They kin use it."

"*Try to say sumpin' funny, Joe.*"

"*I'm the most valuable man in the third wave. Ever'body gave me their cigarettes to carry in my shirt pocket.*"

"I'm lookin' fer turtle eggs, Junior."

"Must be a tough objective. Th' ol' man says we're gonna have th' honor of liberatin' it."

". . . forever, Amen. Hit the dirt!"

"Know any good Moslem prayers? I don't wanna miss any bets."

"Thanks."

"I bet he backfired that thing on purpose."

"Wish to hell I wuzn't housebroke."

"Quiet sector? How ya think I been strikin' matches all day?"

"*I feel like a fugitive from th' law of averages.*"

"I can't git no lower, Willie. Me buttons is in th' way."

"Hell of a patrol. We got shot at."

"*I hate to run on a flat. It tears hell outta th' tires.*"

"*This must look awful suspicious.*"

"*I was beginnin' to think nobody was home.*"

"Wot kind of voices—Brooklyn or guttural?"

"Let B Comp'ny go in. They ain't been kissed yet."

"I made it. I owe ya another fifty bucks."

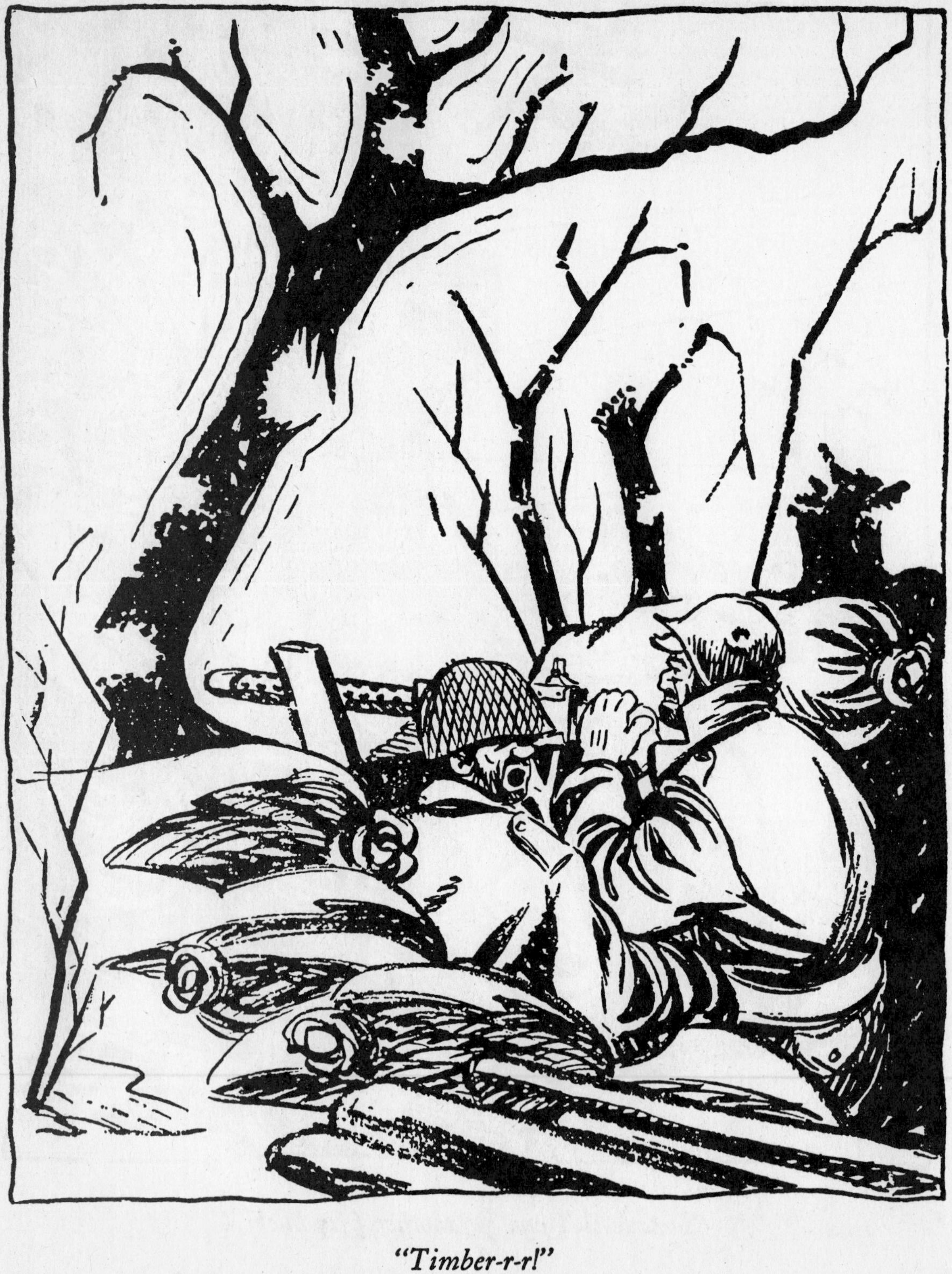

"Timber-r-r!"

"Hope the S.P.C.A. don't hear
about this."

"It sez here, 'Beware of the
dog!' "

"I need a couple of guys what don't owe me no money fer a little routine patrol."

"Able Fox Five to Able Fox. I got a target, but ya gotta be patient."

APOLOGIES TO THE 1st ARMORED DIV.

"We'll go away an' stop botherin' you boys now. Jerry's got our range."

"I'll let ya know if I find th' one wot invented th' 88."

"I'd ruther dig. A movin' foxhole attracks th' eye."

"You gents relax. We got three inches of armor."

"My God! There we wuz an' here they wuz."

"Ever notice th' funny sound these zippers make, Willie?"

Somewhere in Italy

Dear, Dear Miss Mitchell,
    You will probably think this is an
awful funny letter to get from a soldier,
but I was carrying your big book, "Gone
with the Wind," under my shirt, and a

"Dammit, Willie—it wasn't yer turn!"

"Congratulations. You're the 100th soldier who has posed with that bottle of Icy Cola. You may drink it."

"Heck, it's last month's paper. That rear guard on 139 shoulda heard about it by now."

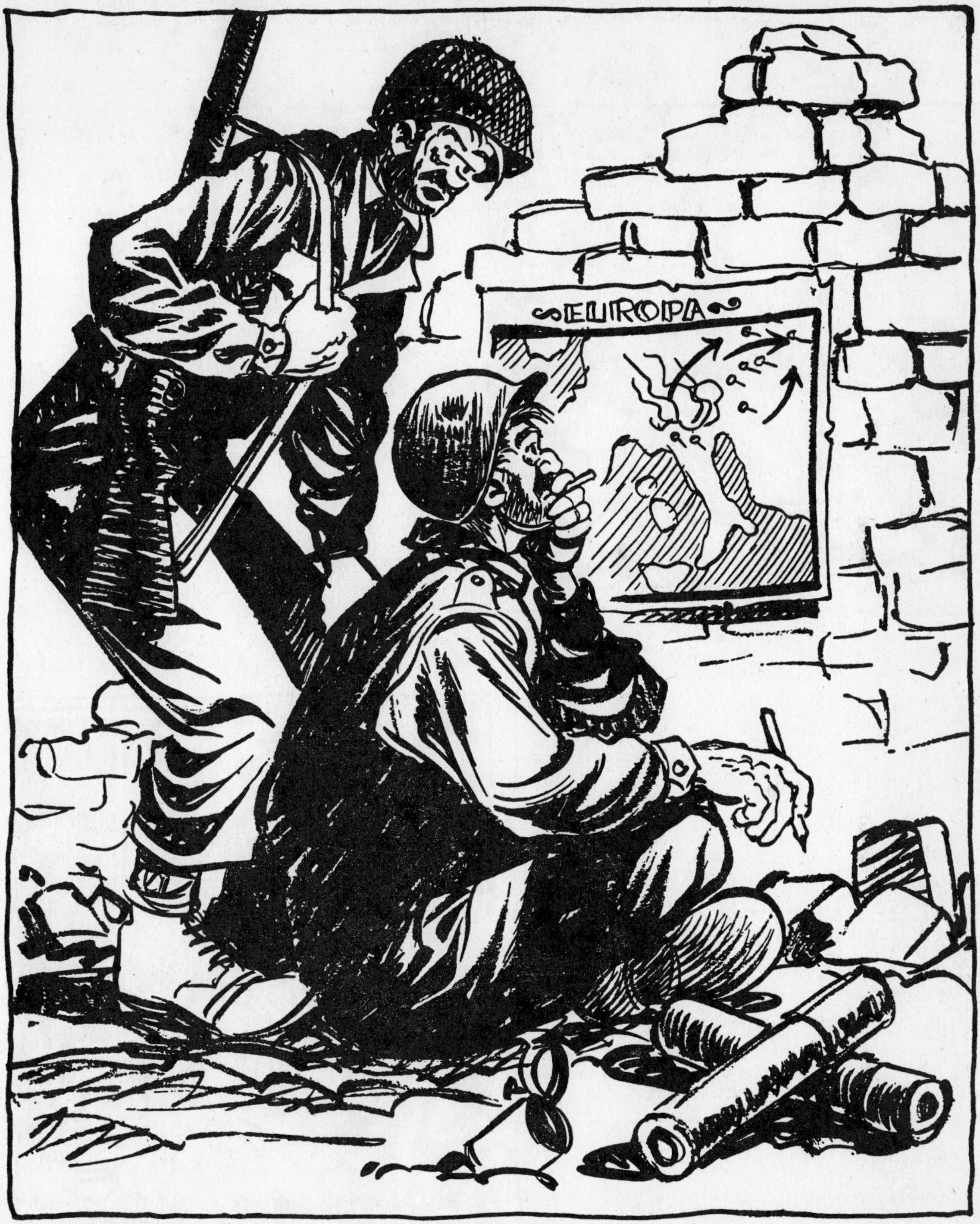
EUROPA

". . . armchair strategist!"

"Sure they's a revolution in Germany. Git down so they won't hit ya wit' a wild shot."

"We just landed. Do you know any good war stories?"

"Th' hell this ain't th' most important hole in th' world. I'm in it."

"When they run we try to ketch 'em. When we ketch 'em we try to make 'em run."

"Maybe Joe needs a rest. He's talkin' in his sleep."

"I see Comp'ny E got th' new style gas masks, Joe."

"Ya won't have any trouble pickin' up our trail after th' first five miles."

Fresh, spirited American troops, flushed with victory, are bringing in thousands of hungry, ragged, battle-weary prisoners. (News item)

"She must be very purty. Th' whole column is wheezin' at her."

"Ya wouldn't git so tired if ya didn't carry extra stuff. Throw the joker outta yer deck o' cards."

"How ya gonna find out if they're fresh troops if ya don't wake 'em up an' ask?"

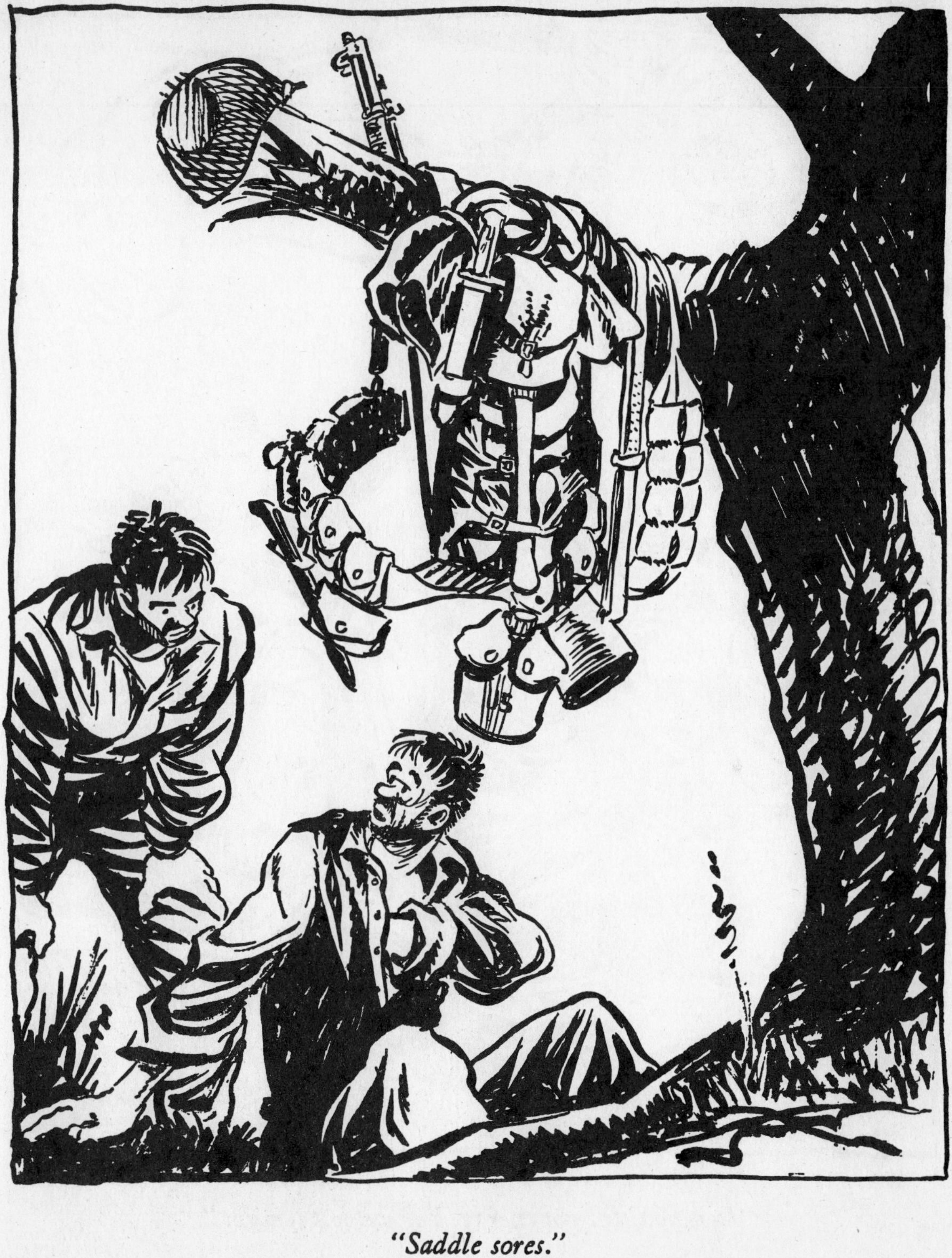

"Saddle sores."

"I see you still got energy. Yer outpost tonight."

"Tell th' ol' man I'm sittin' up wit' two sick friends."

"Hullo, glamorous."
"Howdy, Blitzkrieg."

"Do retreatin' blisters hurt as much as advancin' blisters?"

"We'll be here quite a while, boys. You kin take yer shoes off tonight."

"I wanna long rest after th' war. Mebbe I'll do a hitch in th' reg'lars."

"I'm depending on you old men to be a steadying influence for the replacements."

"Gimme my canteen back, Willie. I see ya soakin' yer beard full."

"You have completed your fiftieth combat patrol. Congratulations. We'll put you on mortars a while."

"Yer lucky. Yer learnin' a trade."

"Yessir—Ol' B Comp'ny broke another bridge buildin' record. A kraut regiment is retreatin' across it."

"Me future is settled, Willie. I'm gonna be a perfessor on types o' European soil."

"Yer wild, happy, free life is over. Tomorrer ya start luggin' ammo ag'in."

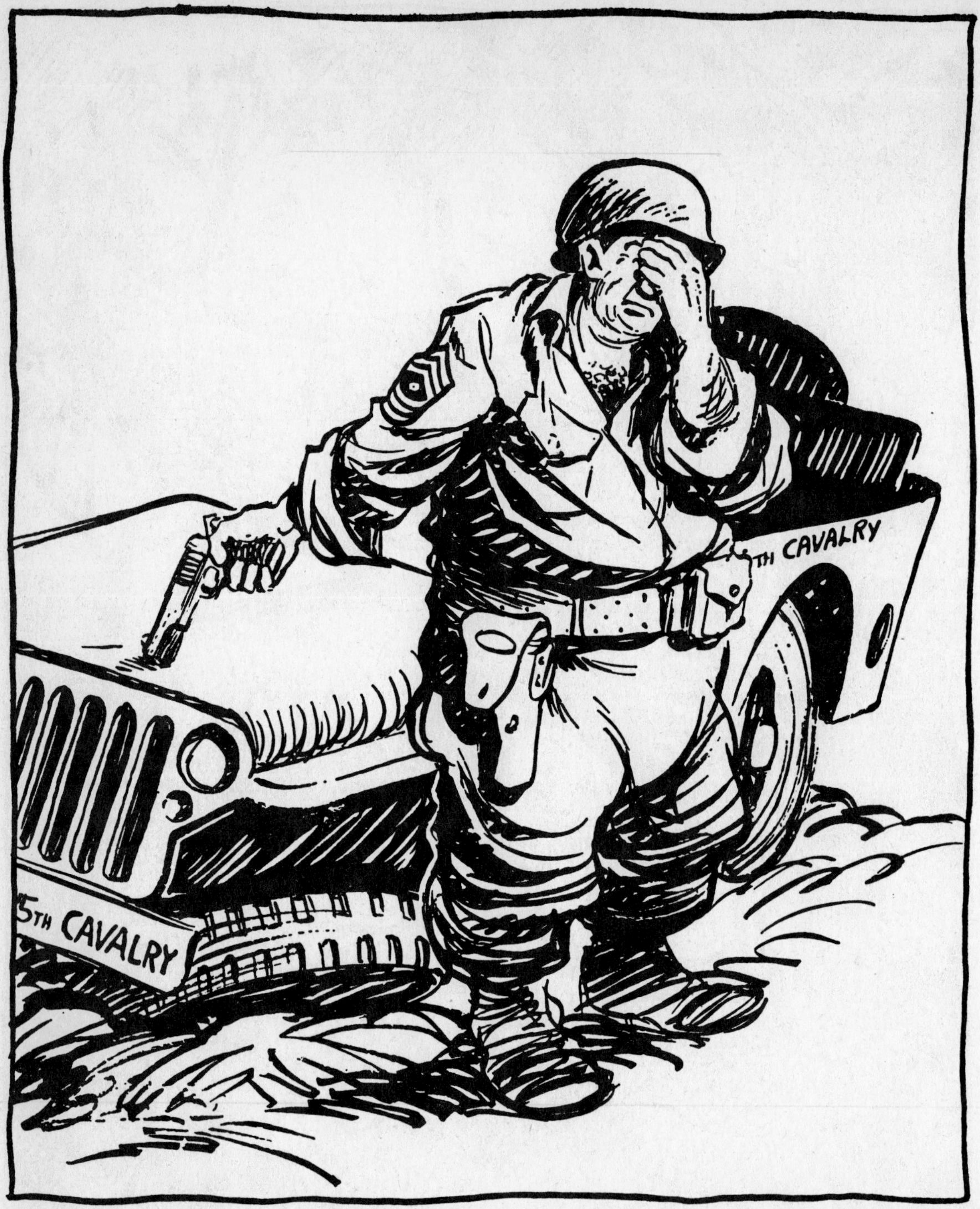
TH CAVALRY
5TH CAVALRY

"Gee, I didn't realize how rough you boys lived on th' ground."

*"The battery is outta H.E., Joe
—kin you use a couple tons of
leaflets?"*

*"Ordnance? Ah'm havin' trou-
ble with mah shootin' ar'n."*

"Tell them leaflet people th' krauts ain't got time fer readin' today."

"K Comp'ny artillery commander speakin'."

*"Among other things, we got a O.P. askin' th' ration dump fer artillery fire, an'
air liaison is tellin' AMG it's too cloudy fer fighter cover."*

"Didn't we meet at Cassino?"

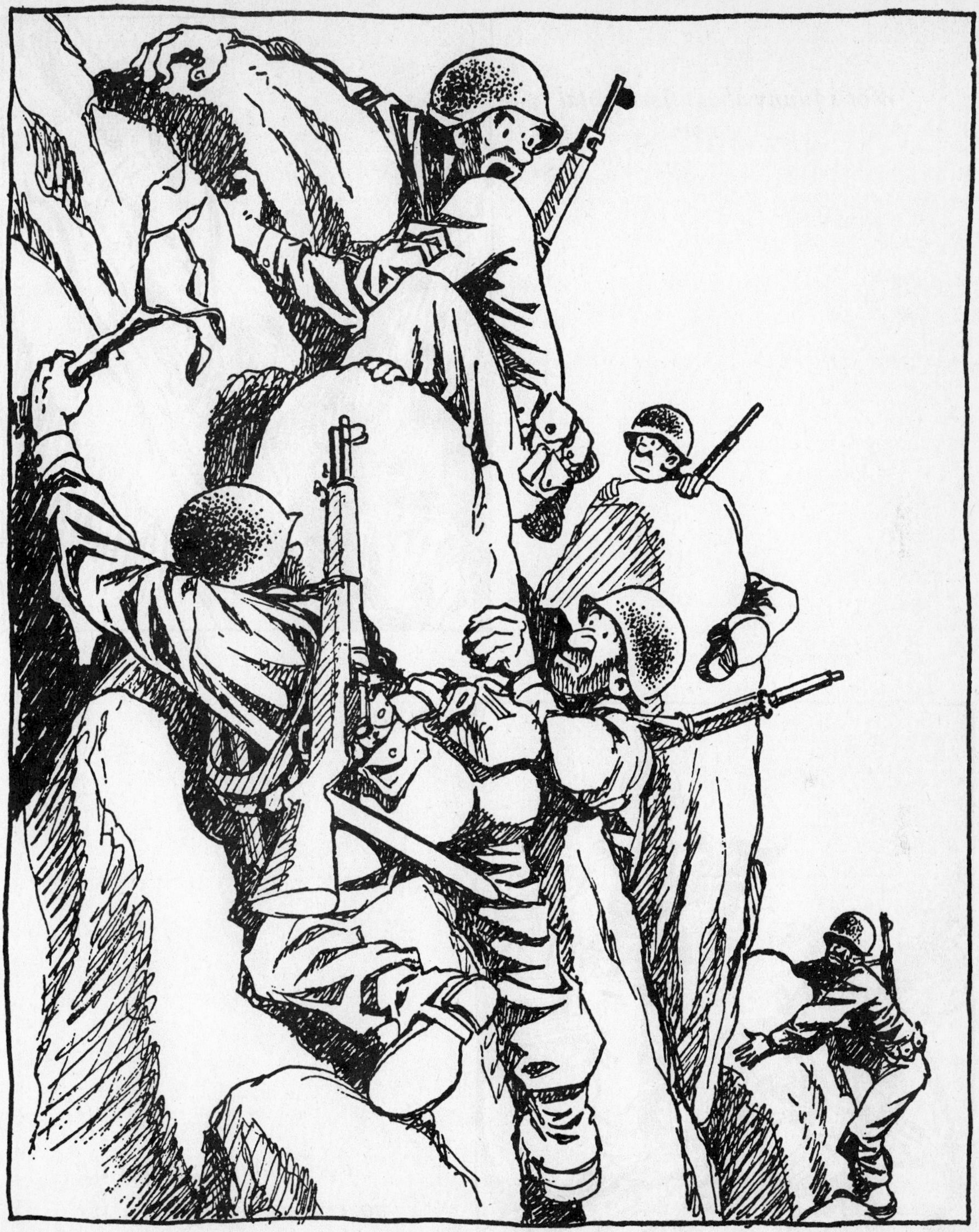

"Hit th' dirt, boys!"

"*Wot's funny about horizontal foxholes?*"

"*I don't haul no water up no crummy mountain fer luxuries.*"

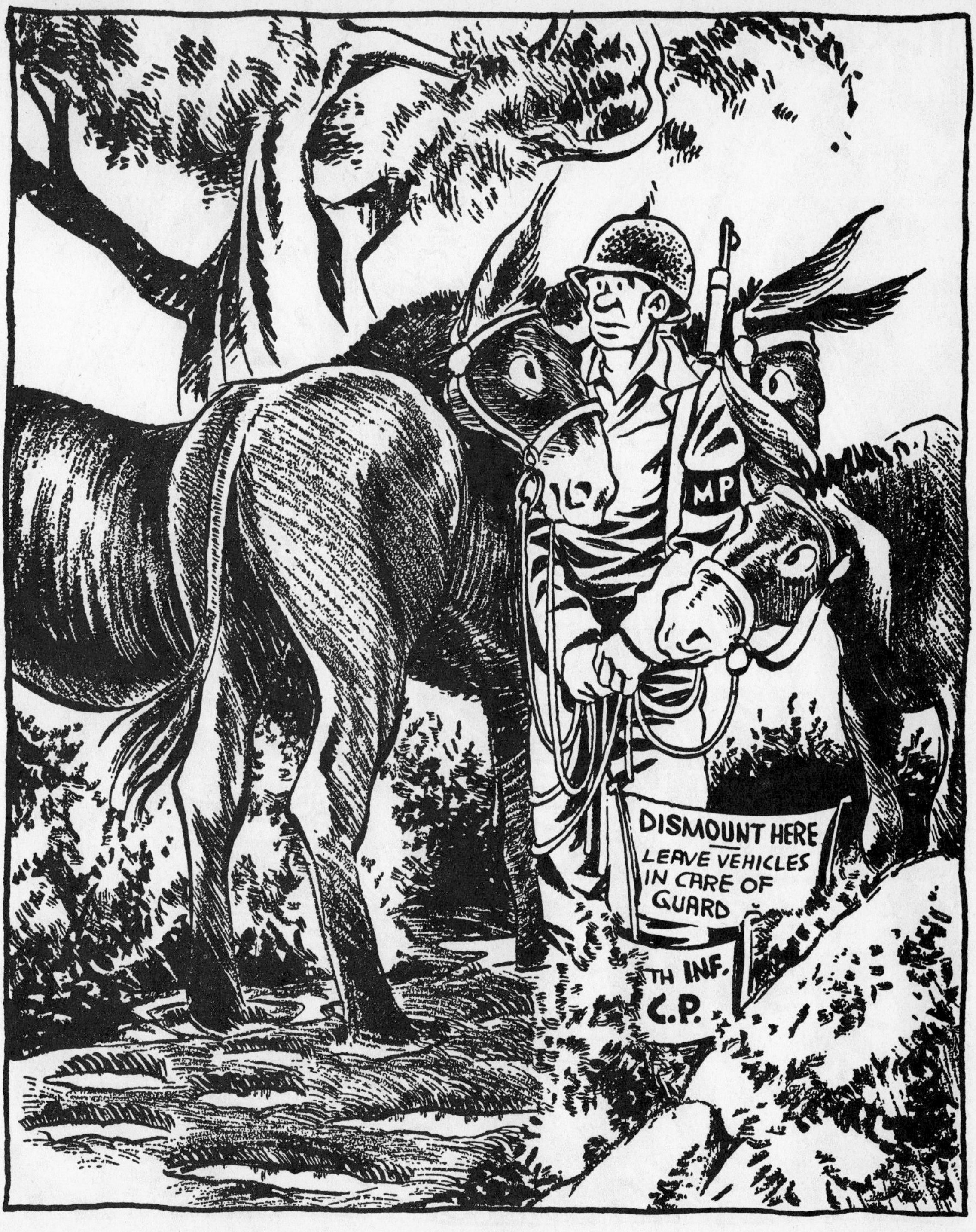
MP
DISMOUNT HERE
LEAVE VEHICLES
IN CARE OF
GUARD
TH INF.
C.P.

"I calls her Florence Nightingale."

"That's our mountain team."

"Hell! Just when I git me practice built up they transfer me to another regiment!"

"I got a hangover. Does it show?"

"It's okay, Joe. I'm a noncombatant."

"Th' boys are beginnin' to think of you as a quack."

"Got anything fer lead poisonin'?"

"I'm jest a country doctor. If ya don't mind, I'll consult with pfc Johnson, th' big blister specialist."

207

"*Quit beefin', or I'll send ya back to th' infantry.*"

"Just gimme th' aspirin. I already got a Purple Heart."

"Who started th' rumor I wuz playin' poker wid a beautiful nurse?"

"Best little mine detector ever made."

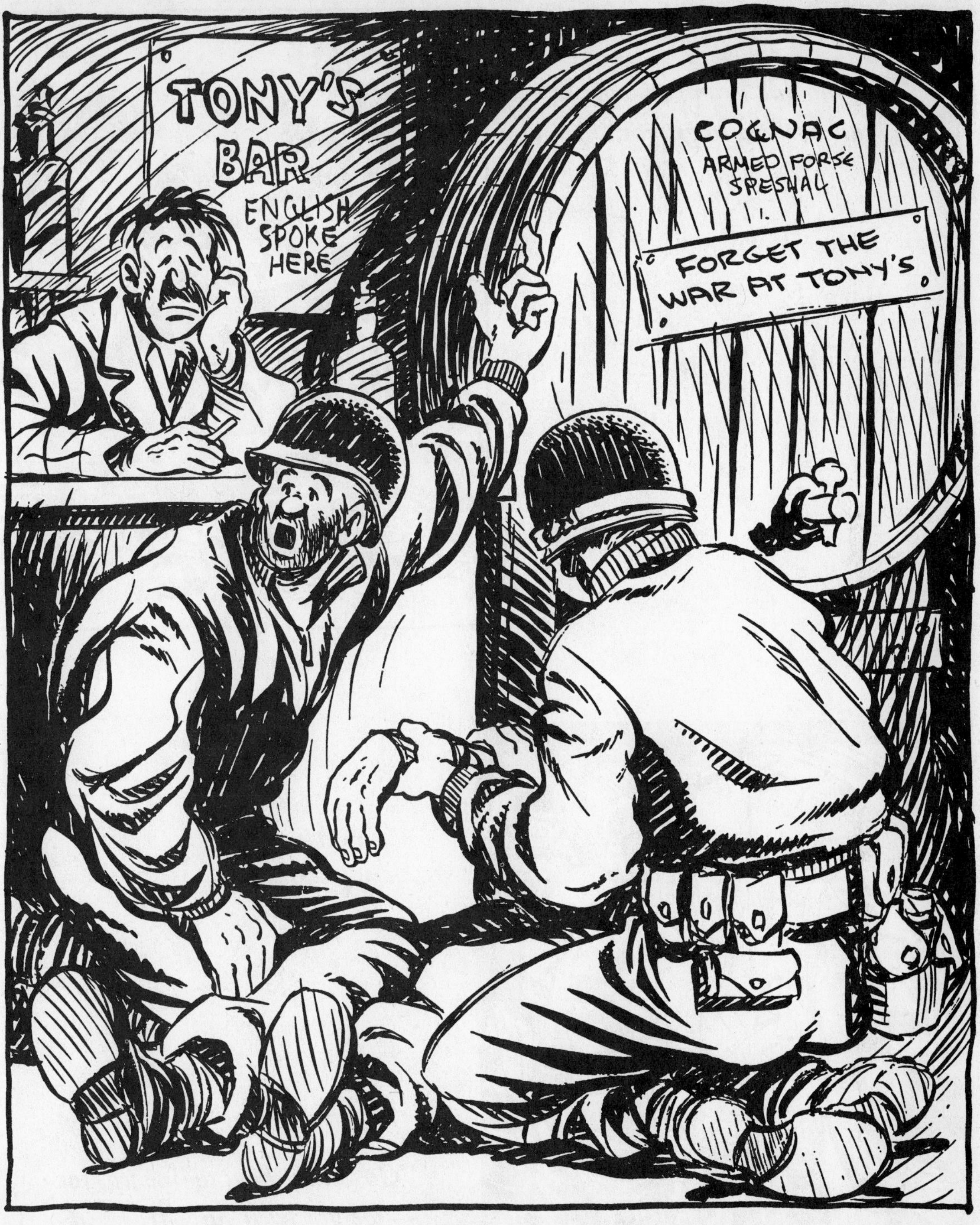
TONY'S BAR
ENGLISH SPOKE HERE
COGNAC
ARMED FORSE SPESHAL
FORGET THE WAR AT TONY'S

"Medics!"

"We shoulda drank th' cognac
an' walked to git gas."

"Go tell th' boys to line up, Joe
—we got fruit juice fer breakfast."

"*We're experimentin' with a new type transfusion.*"

*"Hell of a way to waste time.
Does it work?"*

*"I brung ya a chaser fer all that
plasma, Joe."*

"*We better report we made con-
tack wit' th' enemy an' walked
to our objective.*"

"*Who ever heard of gittin' good
mileage wit' water?*"

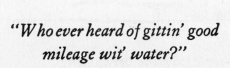

"*We must be retreating, Fritz. They're watering the vermouth.*"

"*Them rats! Them dirty, cold-blooded, soreheaded, stinkin' Huns. Them atrocity commitin' skunks . . .*"

"*Them wuz his exack words—'I envy th' way you dogfaces git first pick o' wimmin an' likker in towns.'*"

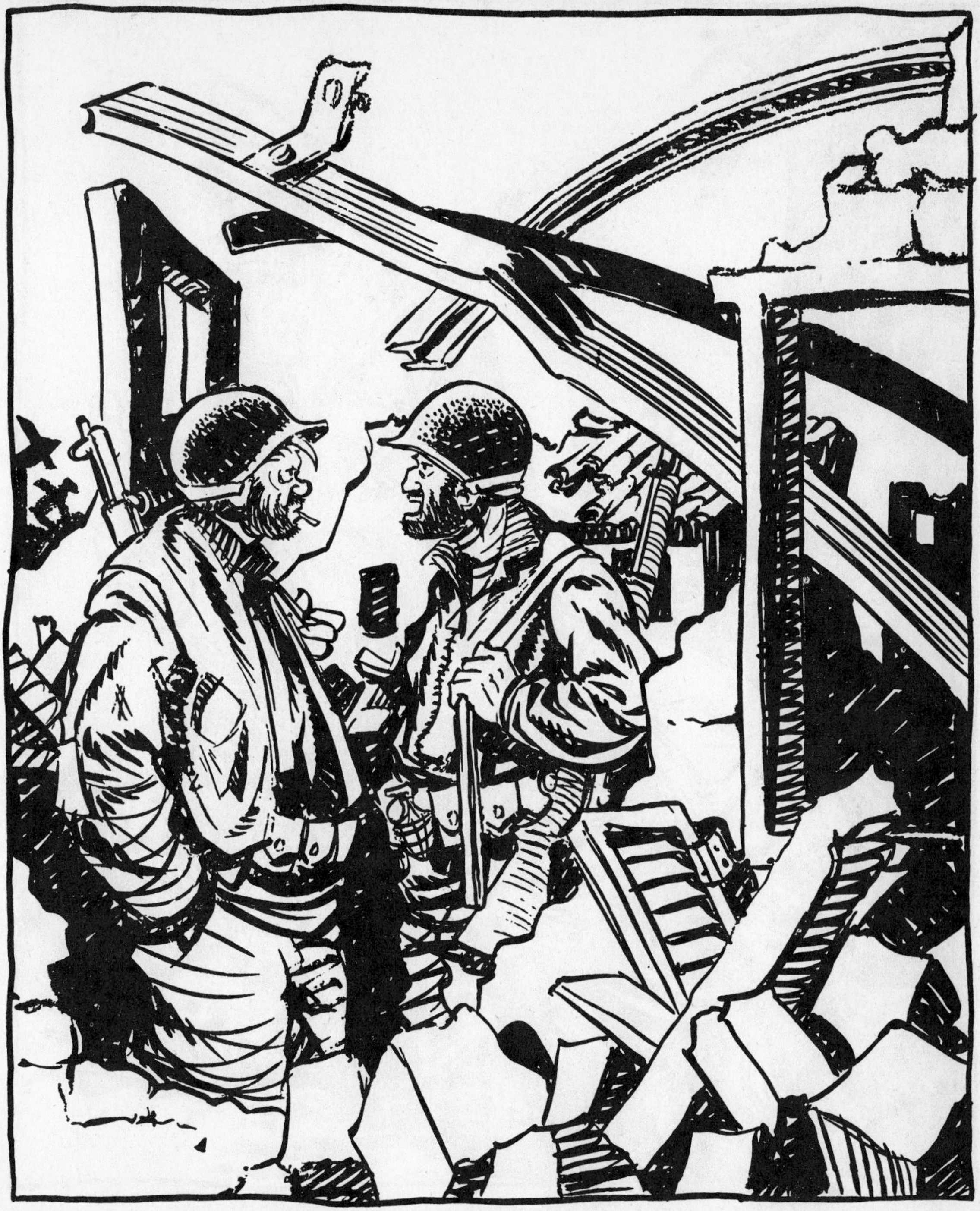

"Let's paint th' town red."

"Don't startle 'im, Joe—it's almost full."

"*Nein, nein—go ahead! I vould not think of interfering.*"

"We're jest a coupla red-blooded American boys."

"Th' krauts ain't followin' ya so good on 'Lili Marlene' to-night, Joe. Ya think maybe somethin' happened to their tenor?"

"My son. Five days old. Good-lookin' kid, ain't he?"

"Why ya lookin' so sad? I got out of it okay."

"So Archibald kissed her ag'in an' gently put her head on th' pillow. She gazed at him wit' half-shut eyes—tremblin' hard—don't forget to buy next week's installment at your newsstand."

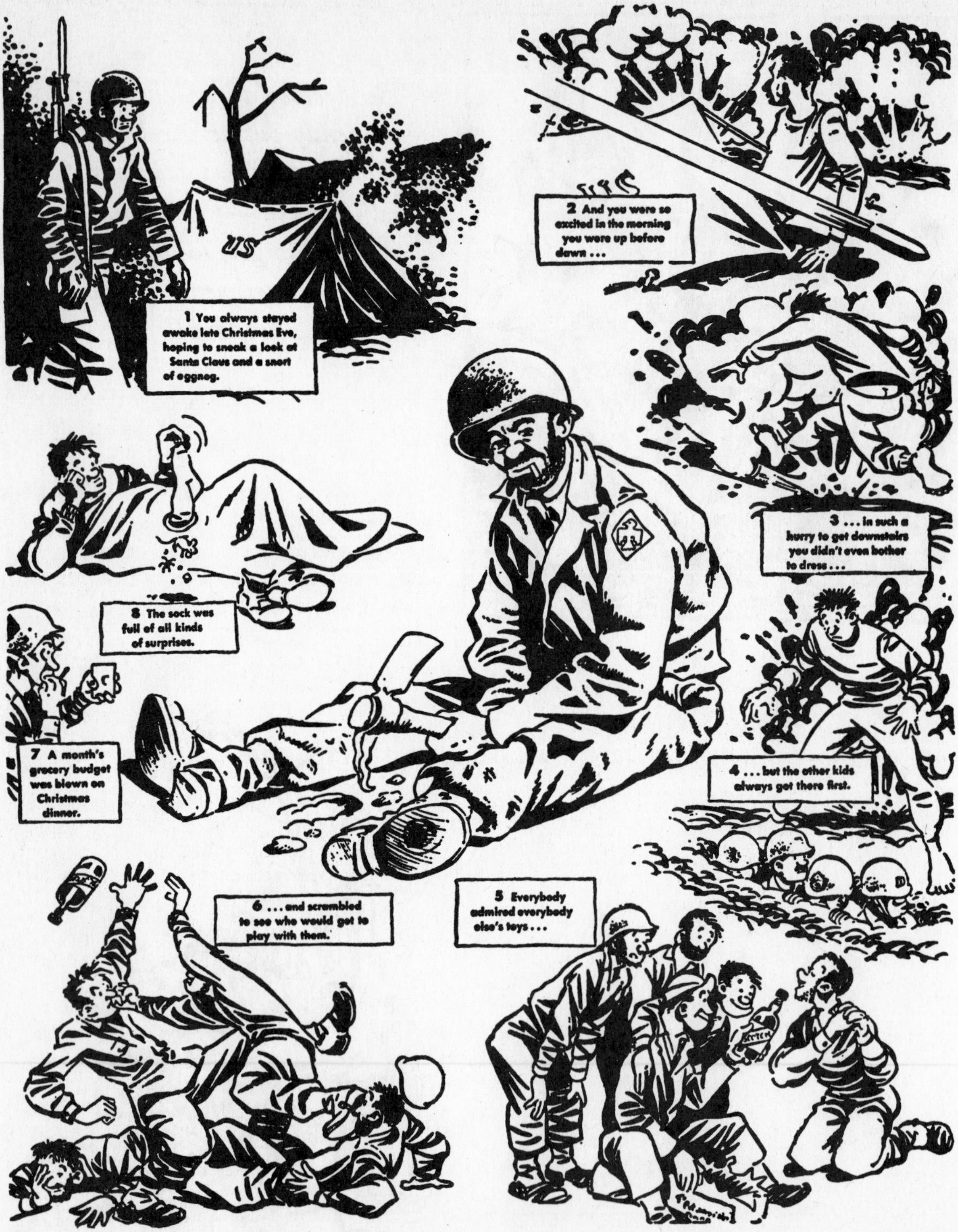
1 You always stayed awake late Christmas Eve, hoping to sneak a look at Santa Claus and a snort of eggnog.
2 And you were so excited in the morning you were up before dawn . . .
3 . . . in such a hurry to get downstairs you didn't even bother to dress . . .
4 . . . but the other kids always got there first.
5 Everybody admired everybody else's toys . . .
6 . . . and scrambled to see who would get to play with them.
7 A month's grocery budget was blown on Christmas dinner.
8 The sock was full of all kinds of surprises.
US

"Git yer mind outta th' gutter."

"It will comfort my ol' woman to know I have gave up rye whisky and ten-cent seegars."

"No parlay Eengleesh."

"Why the hell couldn't you have been born a beautiful woman?"

"You Irish woulda lost this war without allies like Texas and Russia."

"Take off yer hat when ya mention sex here. It's a reverint subject."

"*Are you seeking a company of infantry, mon capitaine?*"

"I ast her to teach me to yodel. She taught me to yodel."

"I'm gonna send this home an' scare my gal outta foolin' around wit' garrison sojers . . ."

"War romance. It won't last."

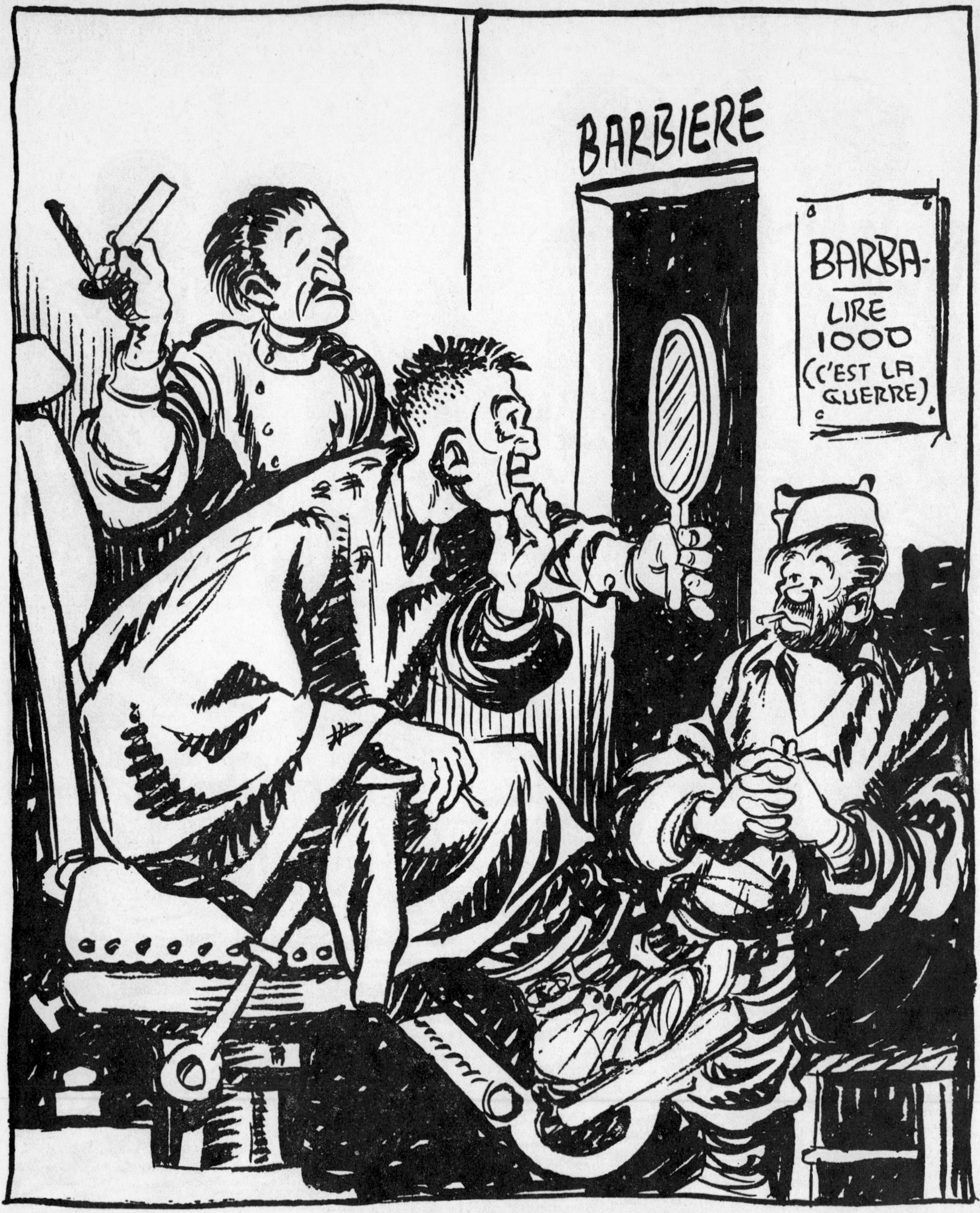
BARBIERE
BARBA-
LIRE
1000
(C'EST LA
GUERRE)

"I'm naked."

"You leeve Weelie alone, or I'll never speak to you again!"

"*Whatsa matta, Joe—you been in France?*"

"*They must have infiltrated during the night.*"

"It's either enemy or off limits."

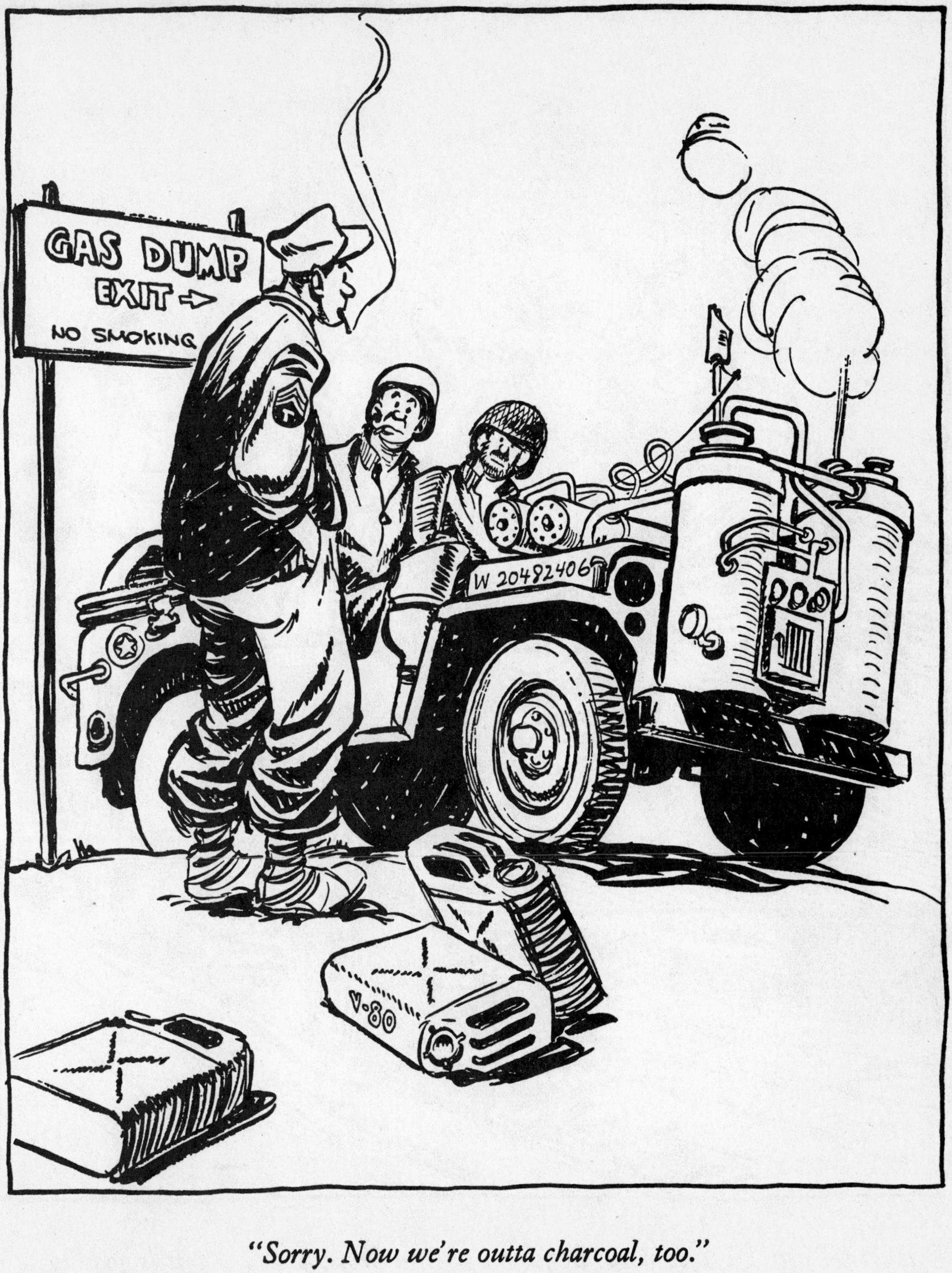
GAS DUMP
EXIT →
NO SMOKING
W 20482406
V-80

"Sorry. Now we're outta charcoal, too."

"Luger, $100 . . . camera, $150 . . . Iron Cross, $12 . . . it is good to be captured by Americans."

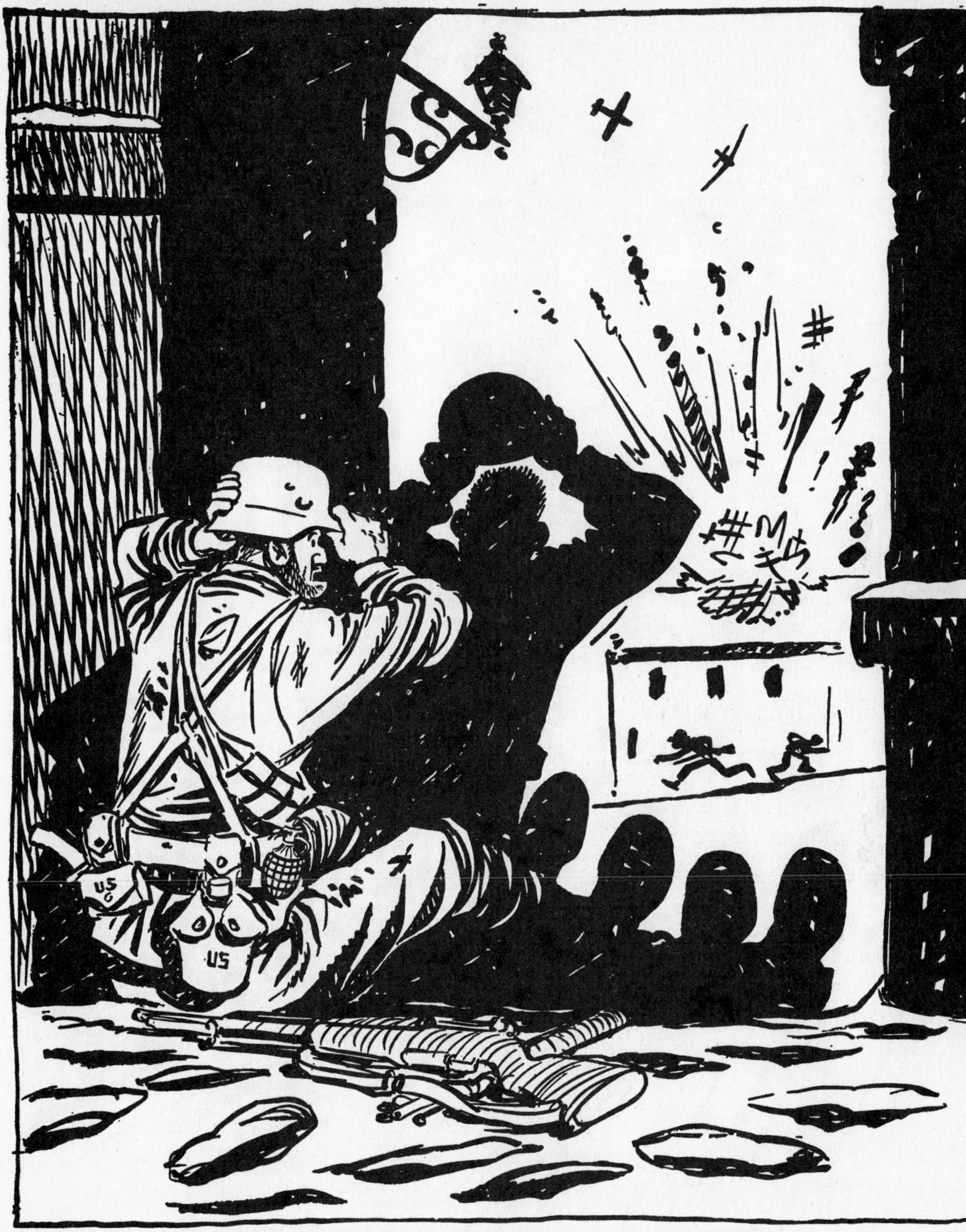
US
US
US

"Sorry. Bad corner!"

"*And now we're entering American territory, old man.*"

"They oughta hire a homme to clean up after them chevaux."

"You blokes leave an awfully messy battlefield."

"This is Fragrant Flower Advance. Gimme yer goddam number."

"I could of swore a couple of krauts wuz usin' that cow for cover, Joe. Go wake up th' cooks."

"We gotta blast 'em out. They found out we feed prisoners C-rations."

"I'll be dawgoned! Did ya know this can opener fits on th' end of a rifle?"

"By th' way—we spotted some kraut gun positions, too."

"*Drop them cans in th' coffee gentle, Joe—we got a chicken stewin' in th' bottom.*"

"*Didn't we meet at th' Cooks
an' Bakers school in '41?*"

"*I caught K.P. ag'in.*"

"Honest, fellers, don't butcher 'im—next time I'll bring five-in-ones!"

"I guess it's okay. The replacement center says he comes from a long line of infantrymen."

"I'm disgusted. I been in th' infantry two days an' I ain't heard a shot."

"Let's grab dis one, Willie. He's packed wit' vitamins."

"*I'm a talent scout fer K Comp'ny. Ya lookin' fer work?*"

"That's right. We're 50 per cent casualty. Joe got nicked."

"Yes, we've sent our quota to the rest camp. . . . This is the company commander speaking!"

"Ya can't git a Expert Infantryman's badge without workin' for it, buddy."

"One of 'em ain't been in long enough. The other has been in too damn long."

"*No, thanks, Willie. I'll go look fer some mud wot ain't been used.*"

"*Aim between th' eyes, Joe . . . sometimes they charge when they're wounded.*"

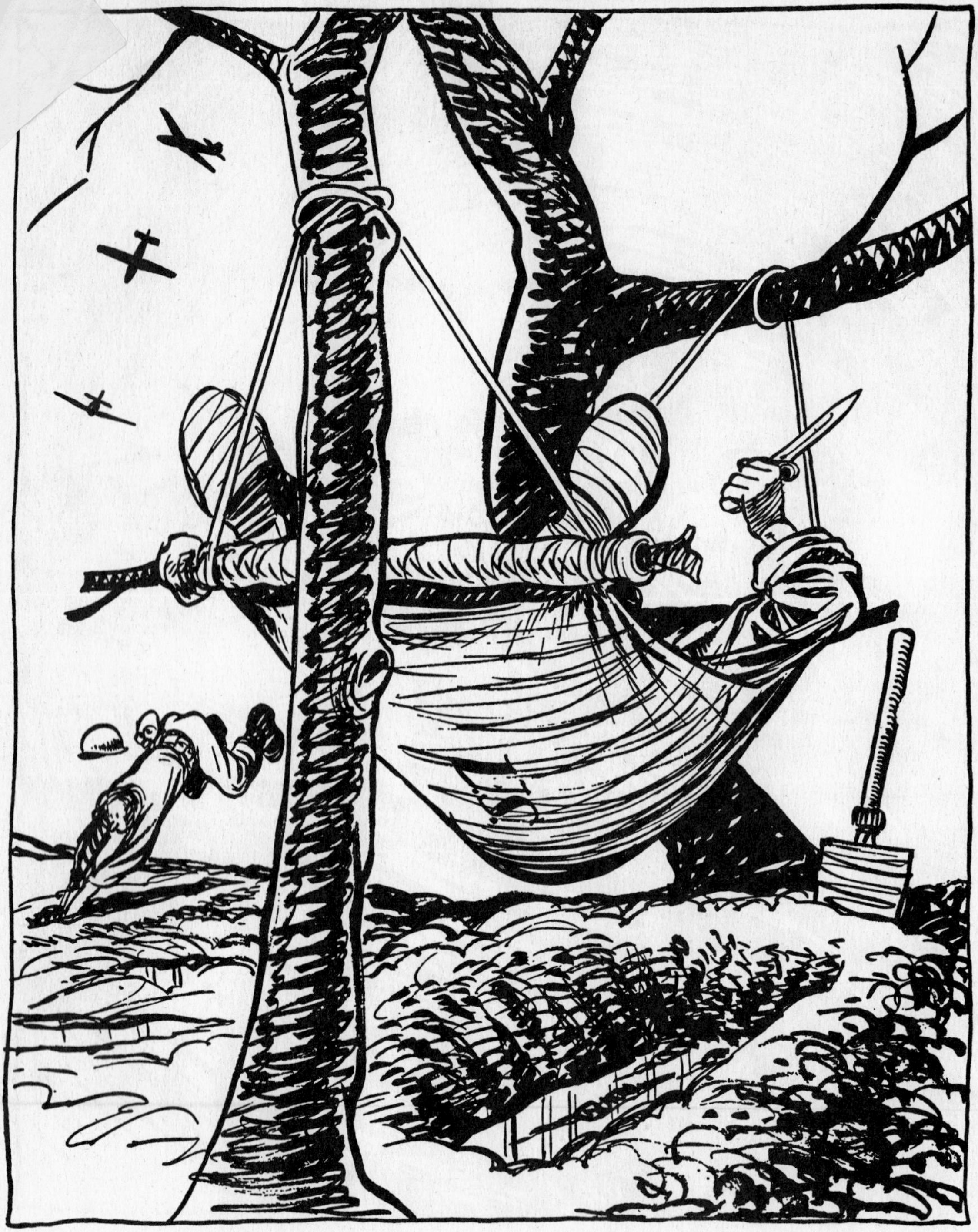

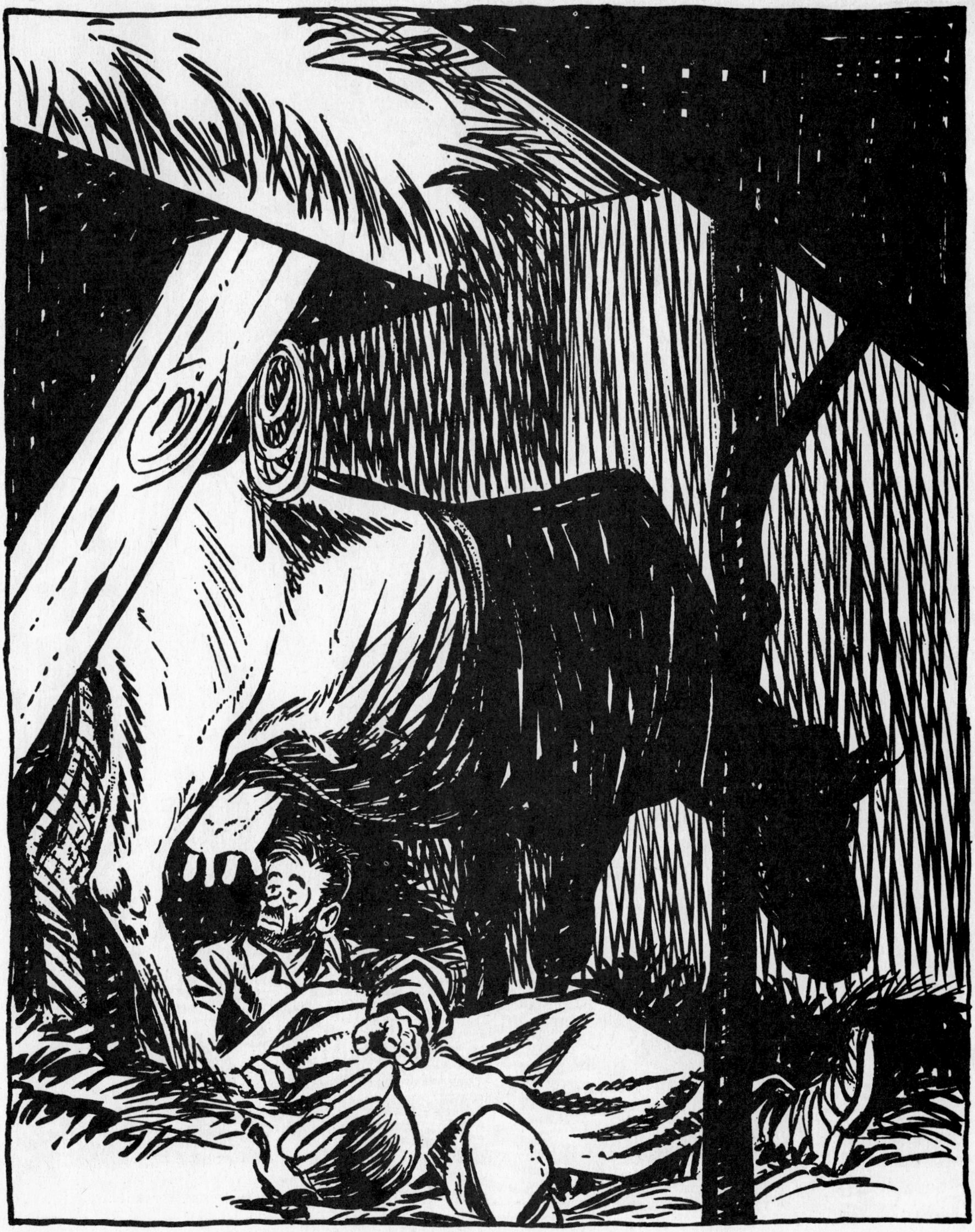

Breakfast in bed

"We gotta probe fer Willie."

"I've given you th' best years o' my life."

"That's th' trouble—mine's fulla cigarettes, too."

"I feels like a pineapple bush."

"It ain't right to go around leanin' on churches, Joe."

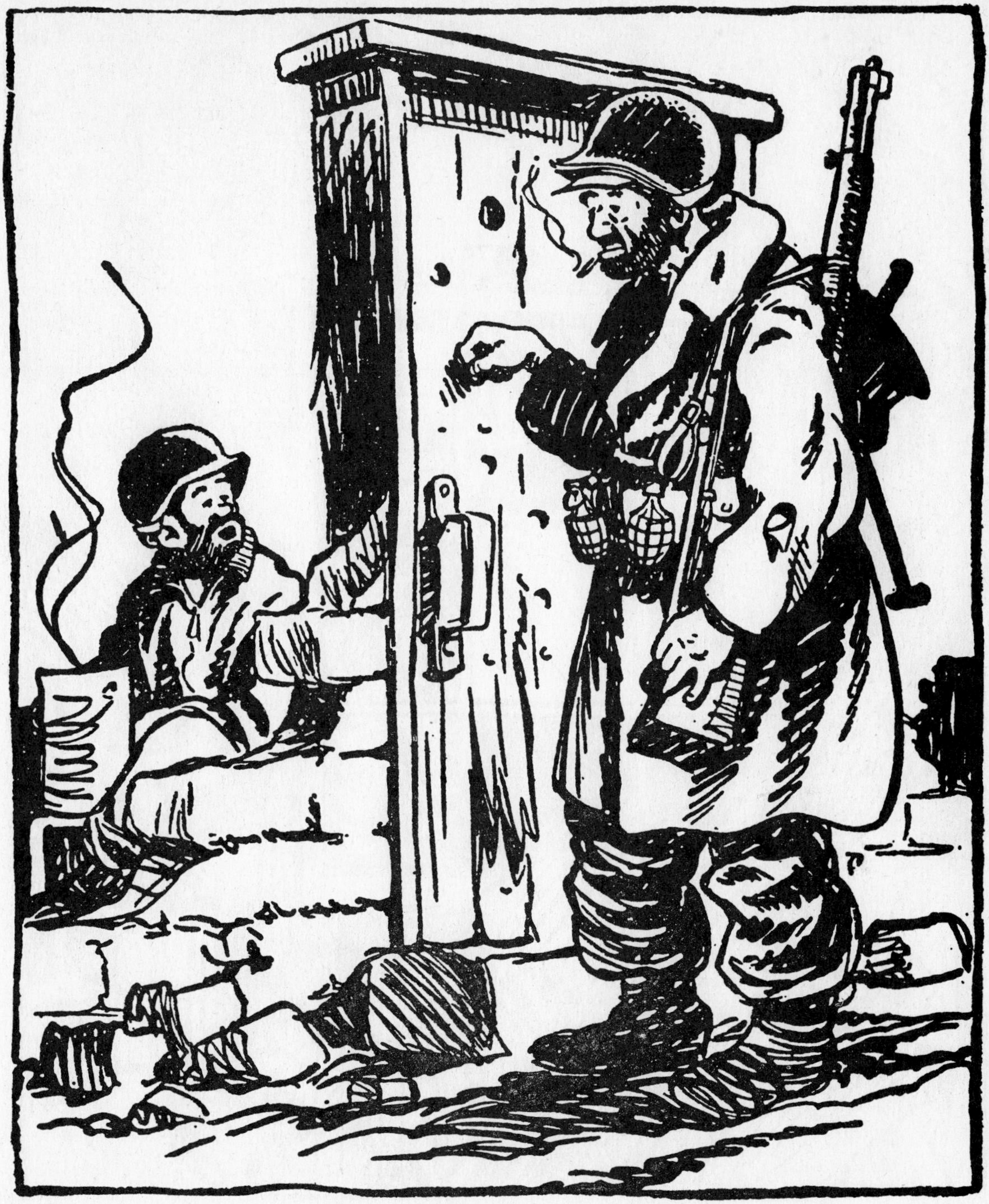

"Who is it?"

"Go ahead, Willie. If ya don't bust it ya'll worry about it all night."

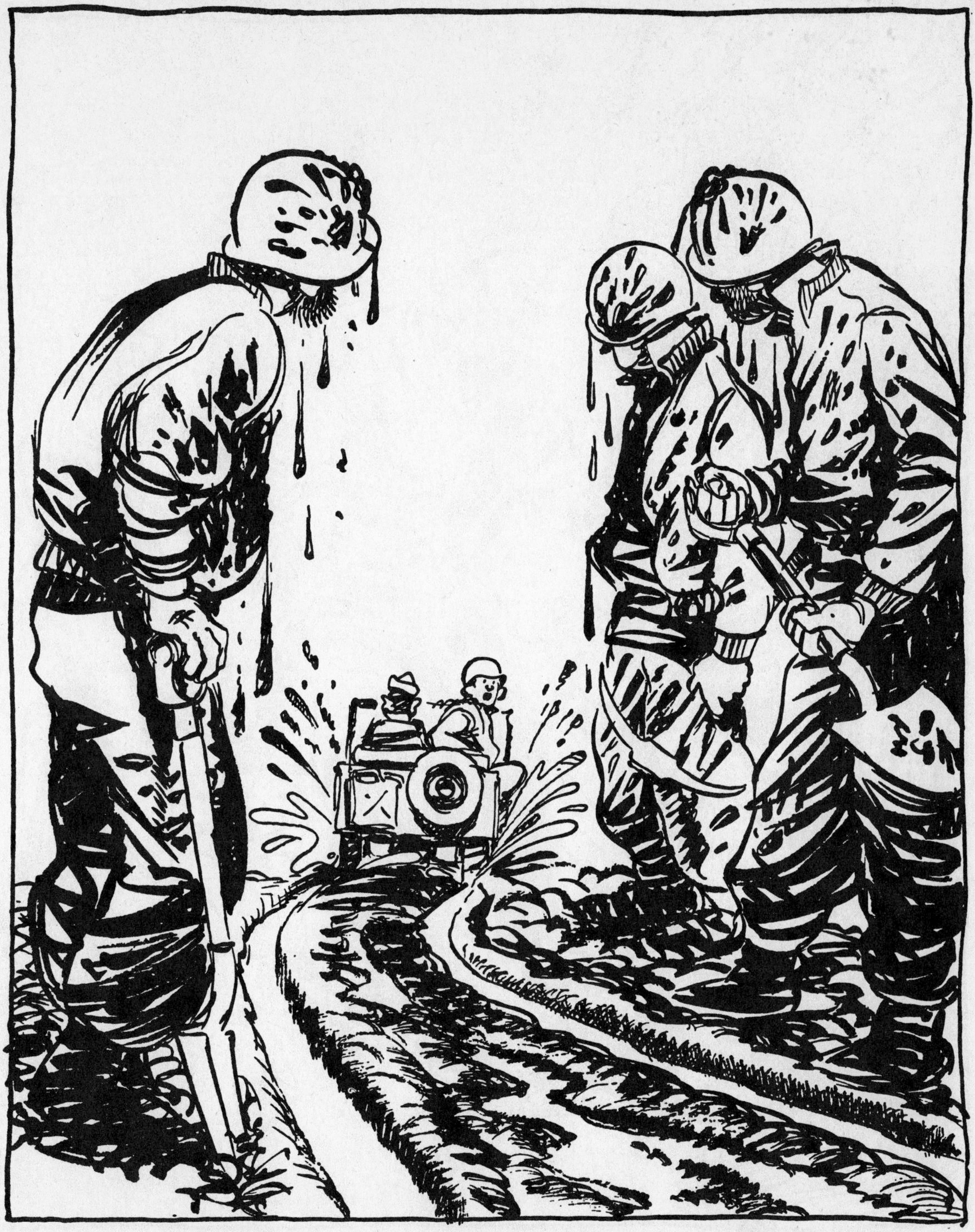

"Damn fine road, men!"

"Awright, awright—it's a gen'ral! Ya wanna pass in review?"

"Hope I meet that guy in civilian life . . ."

"My, sir—what an enthusiastic welcome!"

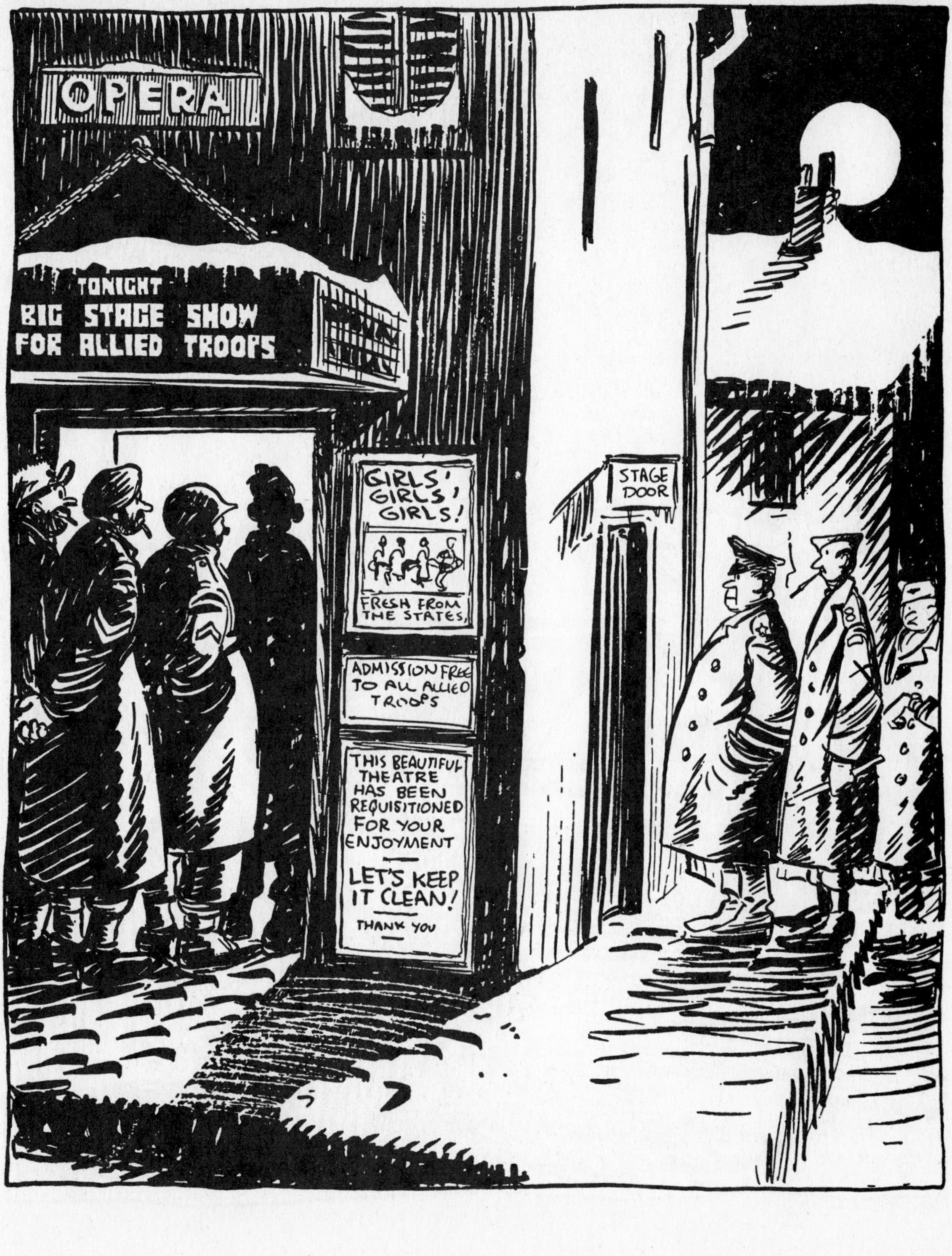
OPERA
TONIGHT
BIG STAGE SHOW
FOR ALLIED TROOPS
GIRLS' GIRLS' GIRLS!
FRESH FROM THE STATES
ADMISSION FREE TO ALL ALLIED TROOPS
THIS BEAUTIFUL THEATRE HAS BEEN REQUISITIONED FOR YOUR ENJOYMENT
LET'S KEEP IT CLEAN!
THANK YOU
STAGE DOOR

"Another dang mouth to feed."

"Don't hurry for me, son. I like to see young men take an interest in their work."

"Beautiful view! Is there one for the enlisted men?"

"One more crack like that an' you won't have yer job back after th' war."

"Dammit, ya promised to bring rations this trip!"

"*Thank you, sir—all we needed wuz somebody blowin' his horn.*"

"I got a pitiful letter from your wife, Soldier. You better give her an allotment after I pay you back that loan."

"I'll *talk to th'* colonel—you ain't gittin' paid to think."

"I tried one of them labor-management argyments wit' Lootenant Atkins."

"Oh, I likes officers. They make me want to live till th' war's over."

"Nice goin', Joe. Now you go take a rest while I finish diggin' my hole."

287

"Tell them prisoners to act sloppier in front of th' lootenant. He might start gittin' ideas."

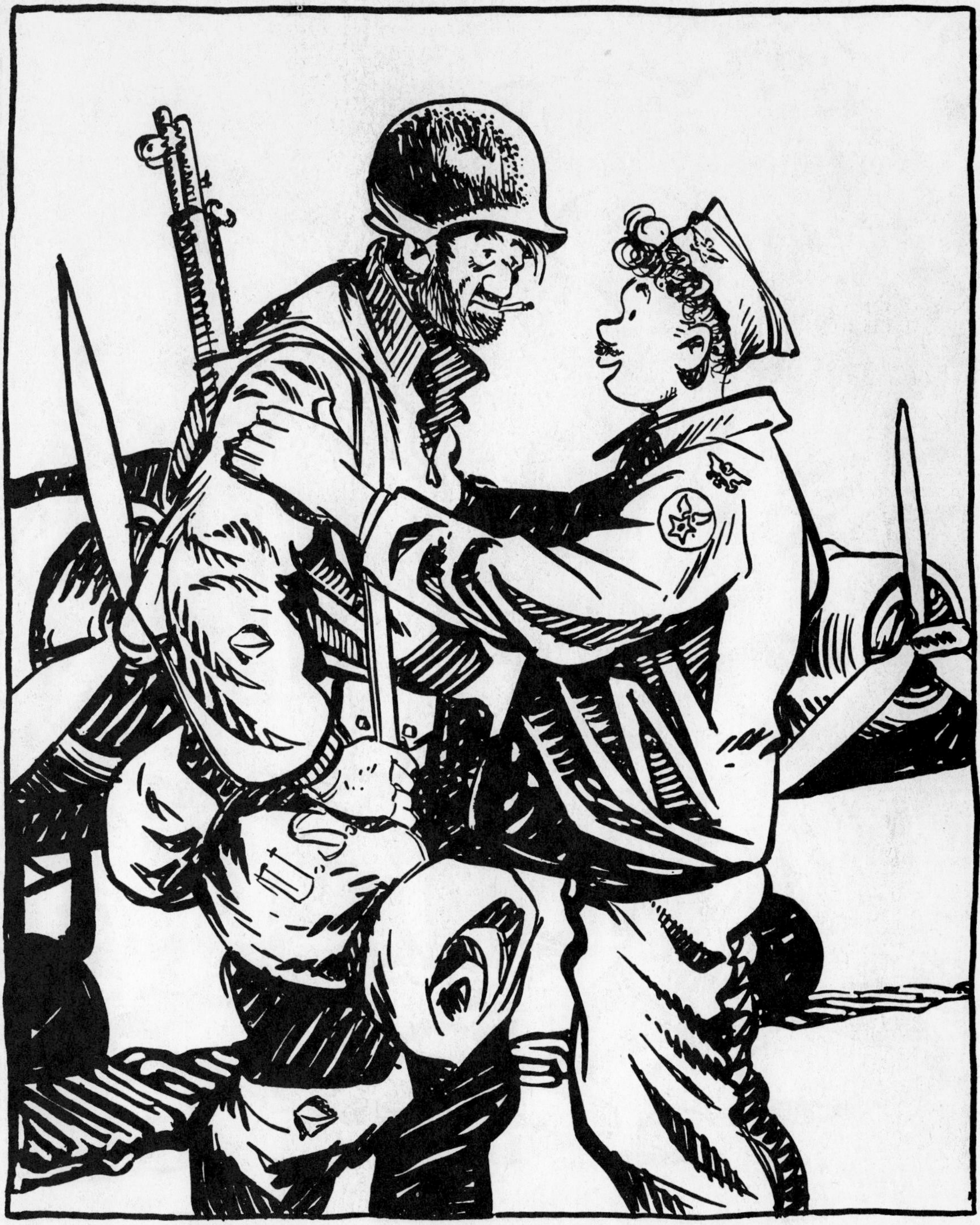

"Uncle Willie!"

"You'll git over it, Joe. Oncet I wuz gonna write a book exposin' th' Army after th' war, myself."

"Your citation went through, Joe."

"He's already gittin' drunk wit' power."

"Let's step it up, Sergeant—we want to get there in time for a long rest."

293

"Sure I got seniority. I got busted a week before you did."

"Honest, pal—they done it to me while I wuz unconscious!"

"I beg yer pardon. I didn't know ya wuz a captain at Culver."

"By God, sir, I tried!"

"Whistle if you see anybody coming . . ."

"*Straighten those shoulders! How long have you been in the Army?*"

"Ya might hafta catch a boat. One of them kids ya chased off th' field
wuz the pilot."

"Don't tell 'em now, Lootenant. Wait'll they fix th' stove."

"He's pretty sore. He says we didn't even try to capture his cook an' his orderly."

"*Nonsense. S-2 reported that machine gun silenced hours ago. Stop wiggling your fingers at me.*"

"Sir, do ya hafta draw fire while yer inspirin' us?"

"Looks like we're goin' into th' line, Willie."

"Don't mention it, Lootenant. They might have replaced ya with one of them salutin' demons."

*"By th' way, what wuz them changes you wuz gonna make when you took **over** last month, sir?"*

"*Them buttons wuz shot off when I took this town, sir.*"

"If you'll turn my weapons platoon loose, I'll give ya my cooks fer security. We're goin' in th' line tonight."

"Th' hell with it, sir. Let's go back to th' front."

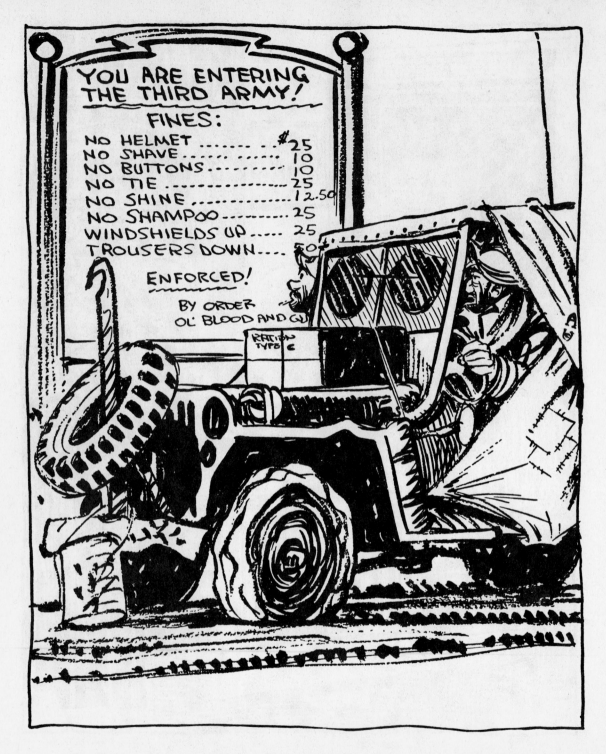

"Radio th' ol' man we'll be late on account of a thousand-mile detour."

"*I think he should at least try to lie at attention.*"

*"We better scram, Willie—th'
Army's movin' in."*

*"Drink it all, boys—th' guy
wot put out that order about
shavin' ain't comin' up here to
inspect us."*

"He says we kin git a room in th' Catacombs. They useta keep Christians in 'em."

"The enemy had a mania for destruction, General. Every elevator cable in town is cut."

"It's best not to speak to paratroopers about saluting. They always ask where you got your jump boots."

"Grab his pistol, Joe—we kin take it to th' rear an' trade it fer some combat boots."

"*We could go to Naples, sir—I know a corporal with a nice apartment.*"

"How's things ın th' States?"

"*Ya must've missed Headquarters on the way up. It's halfway between where the timber stops growin' an' the sojers start shavin'.*"

"Here comes one of them clerks from Corps. Start pickin' yer teeth with a bayonet."

"He's right, Joe. When we ain't fightin' we should act like sojers."

*"We calls 'em garritroopers.
They're too far forward t' wear
ties an' too far back t' git shot."*

*"That can't be no combat man.
He's lookin' fer a fight."*

"Bloody immoral army. They get that red ribbon if they stay out of trouble for a bloody year."

"Th' yellow one is fer national defense, th' red one wid white stripes is fer very good conduct, and th' real purty one wid all th' colors is fer bein' in this theater of operations. . . ."

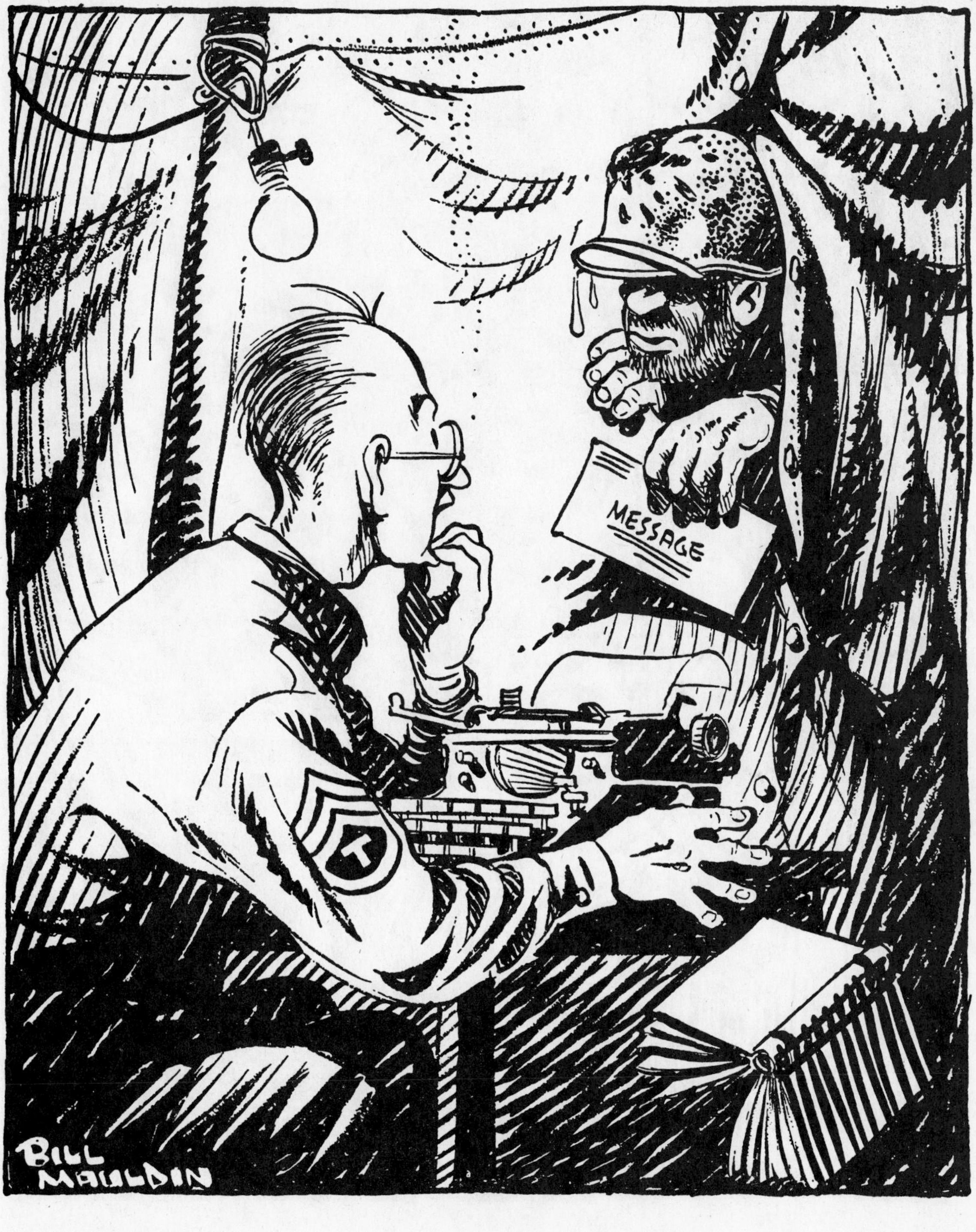
MESSAGE
BILL MAULDIN

"Eeeeeek!"

"So I told Company K they'd just have to solve their own replacement problem."

*"We better stop fillin' in our foxholes when we move up, Willie. Regimental Head-
quarters has been raisin' the devil."*

"Ya don't git combat pay 'cause ya don't fight."

"Here's yer money back fer them souvenirs. You been scarin' hell outta our replacements with yer stories."

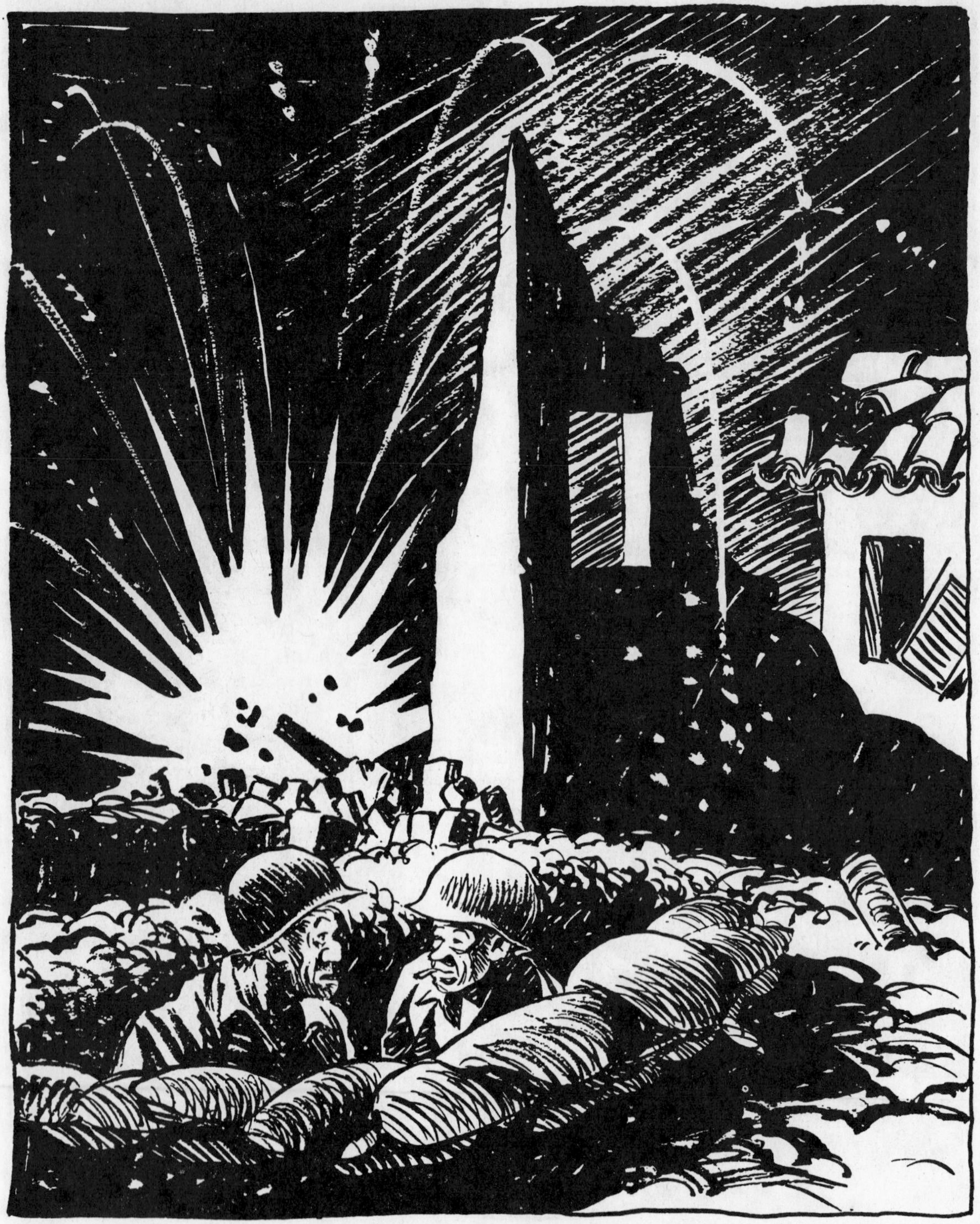

"Did ya volunteer for this or git caught in th' black market?"

(NOTE: In several cases during the Battle of France, supply troops convicted of black-marketeering were given their choice of prison or infantry duty. This was fine punishment and the riflemen were glad to get the replacements, but they were hardly flattered.)

"It's a habit Joe picked up in Rome."

". . . I'll never splash mud on a dogface again (999). . . . I'll never splash mud on a dogface again (1000). . . . Now *will ya help us push?*"

"You'd hurry home too, if you lived in a ration dump."

"I'll be derned. Here's one what wuz wrecked in combat."

"Some of you may not come back. A French convoy has been reported on the road."

"*Tell him to look at th' bright side o' things, Willie. His trees is pruned, his ground is plowed up, an' his house is air-conditioned.*"

"Papa, I think we have been liberated."

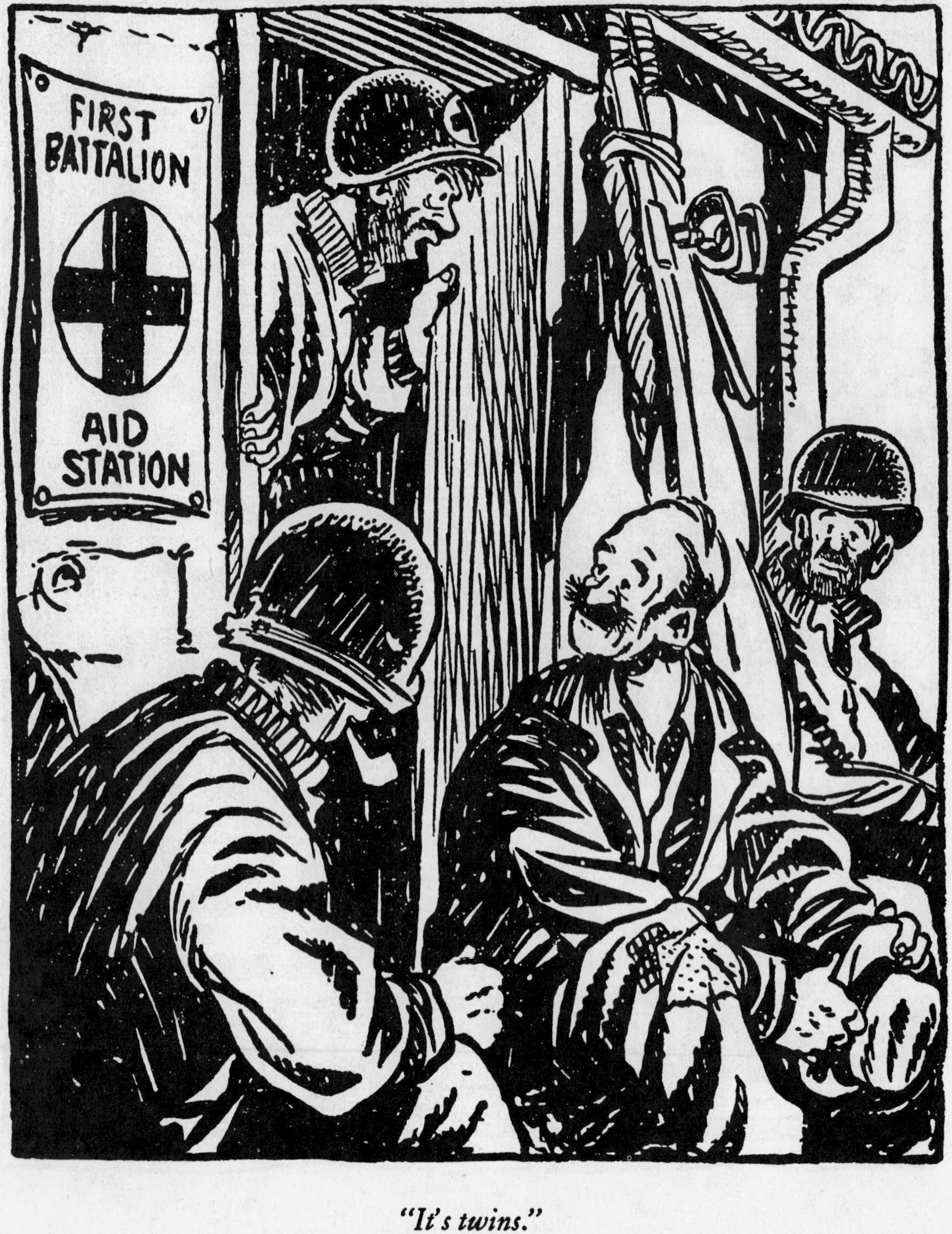
FIRST BATTALION
AID STATION

"It's twins."

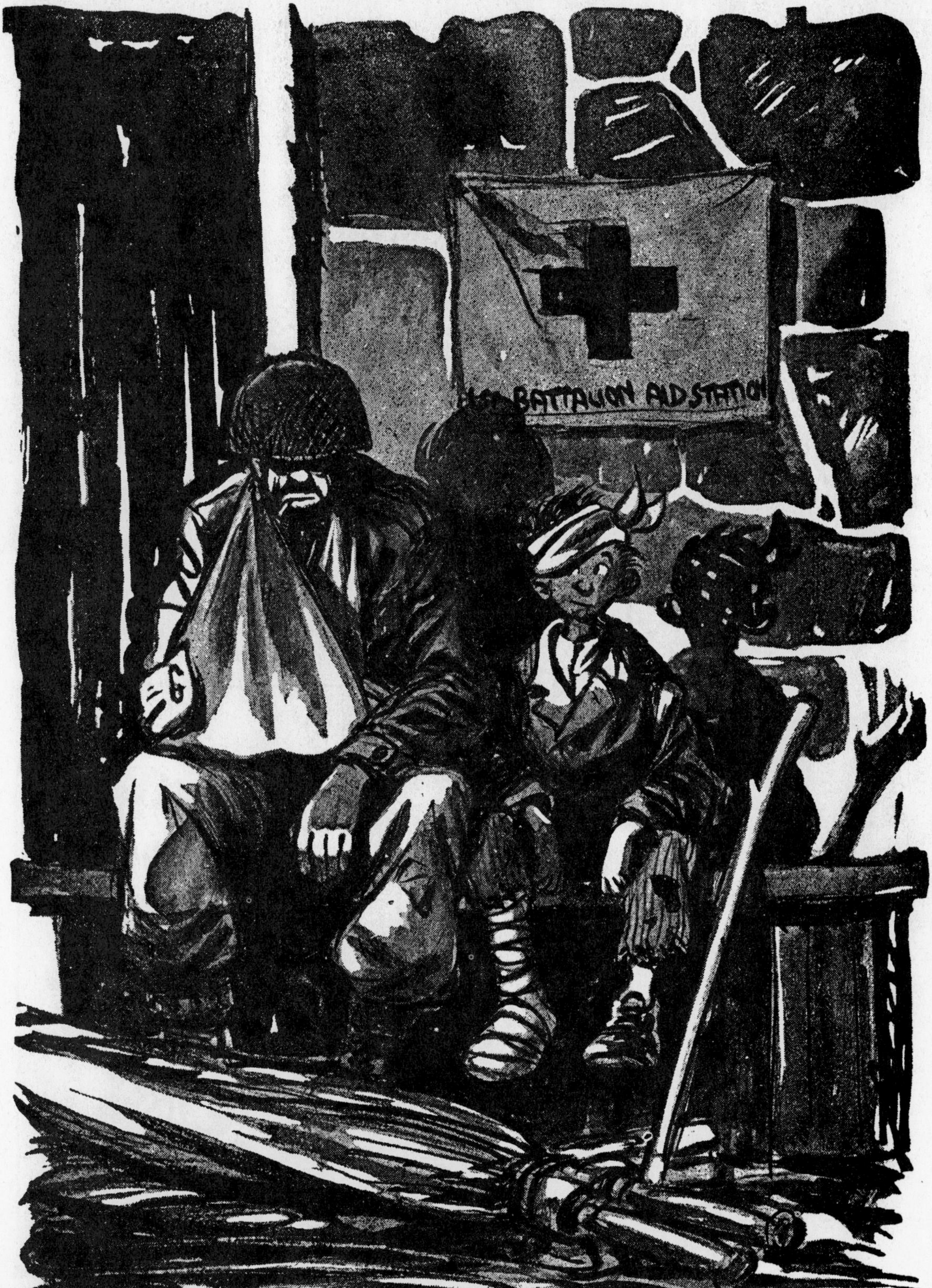
BATTALION AID STATION

"You Americans have everything."

"The restaurants are closed, but you can buy something from the Americans."

"The word for eggs is 'des oeufs.'"

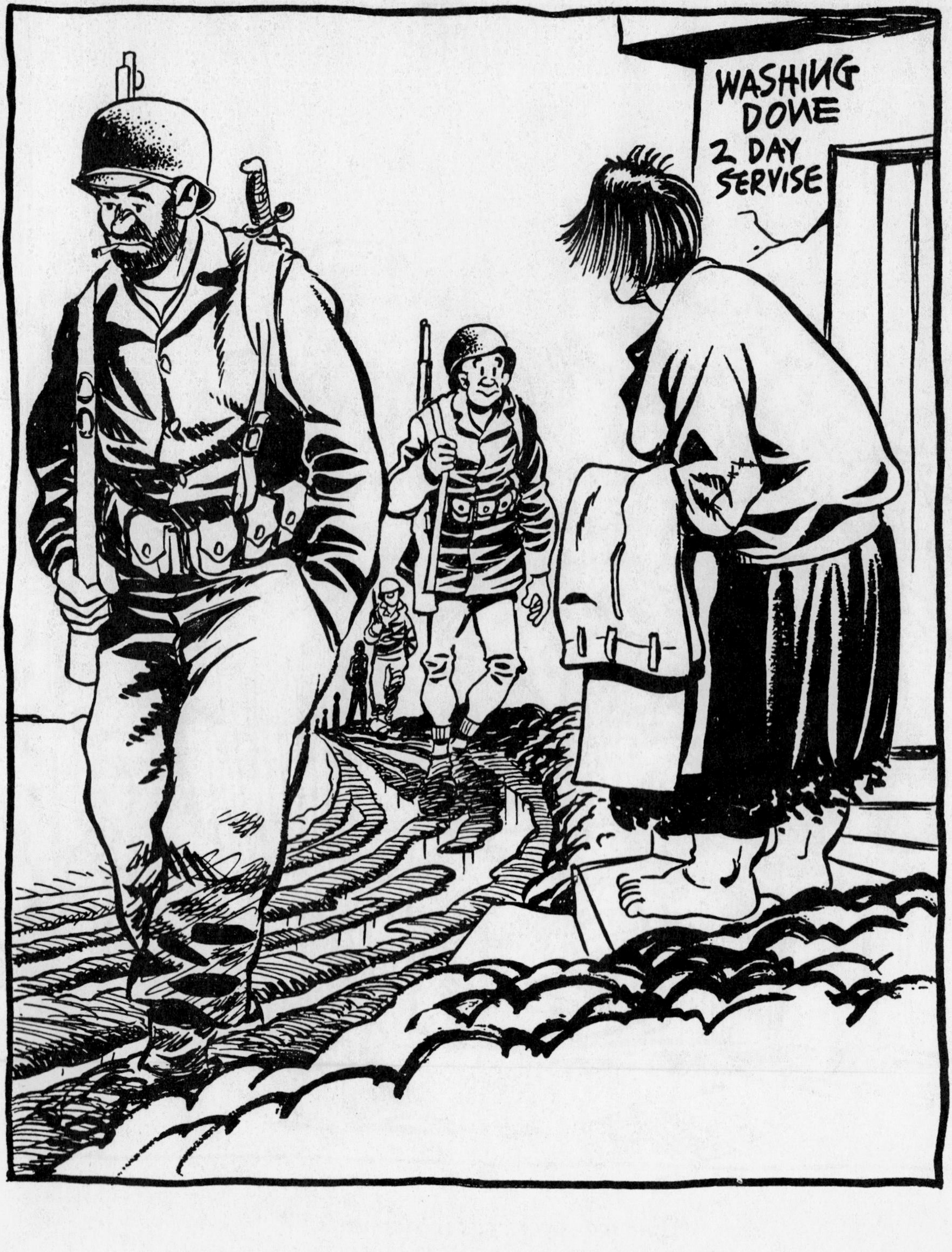
WASHING
DONE
2 DAY
SERVISE

"*Better be careful, Tony. Wait until you're sure the Germans won't counterattack.*"

341

The prince and the pauper

"Feed it, lady. Nobody's lookin'."

"They may be wired to a mine."

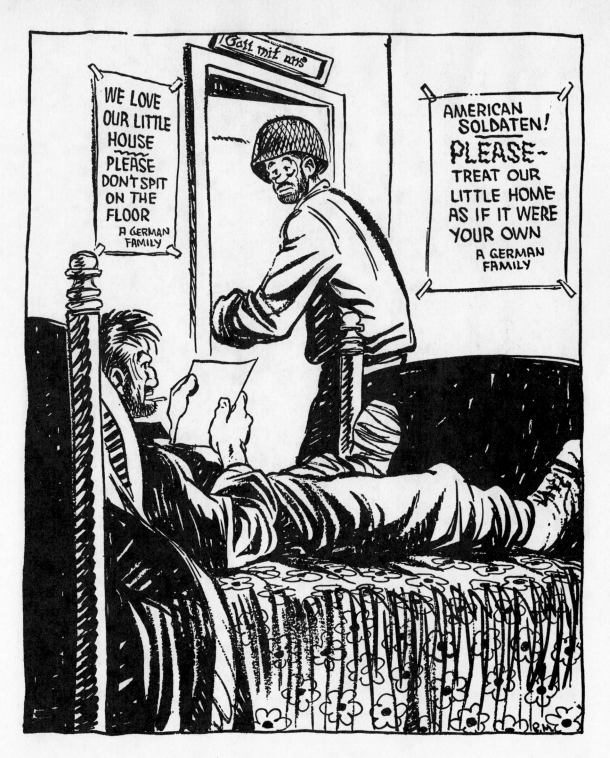

"*Careful. Th' toilet seat's booby-trapped.*"

"Must belong to a politician."

"Follow them, Ilse. Papa's got our ration book."

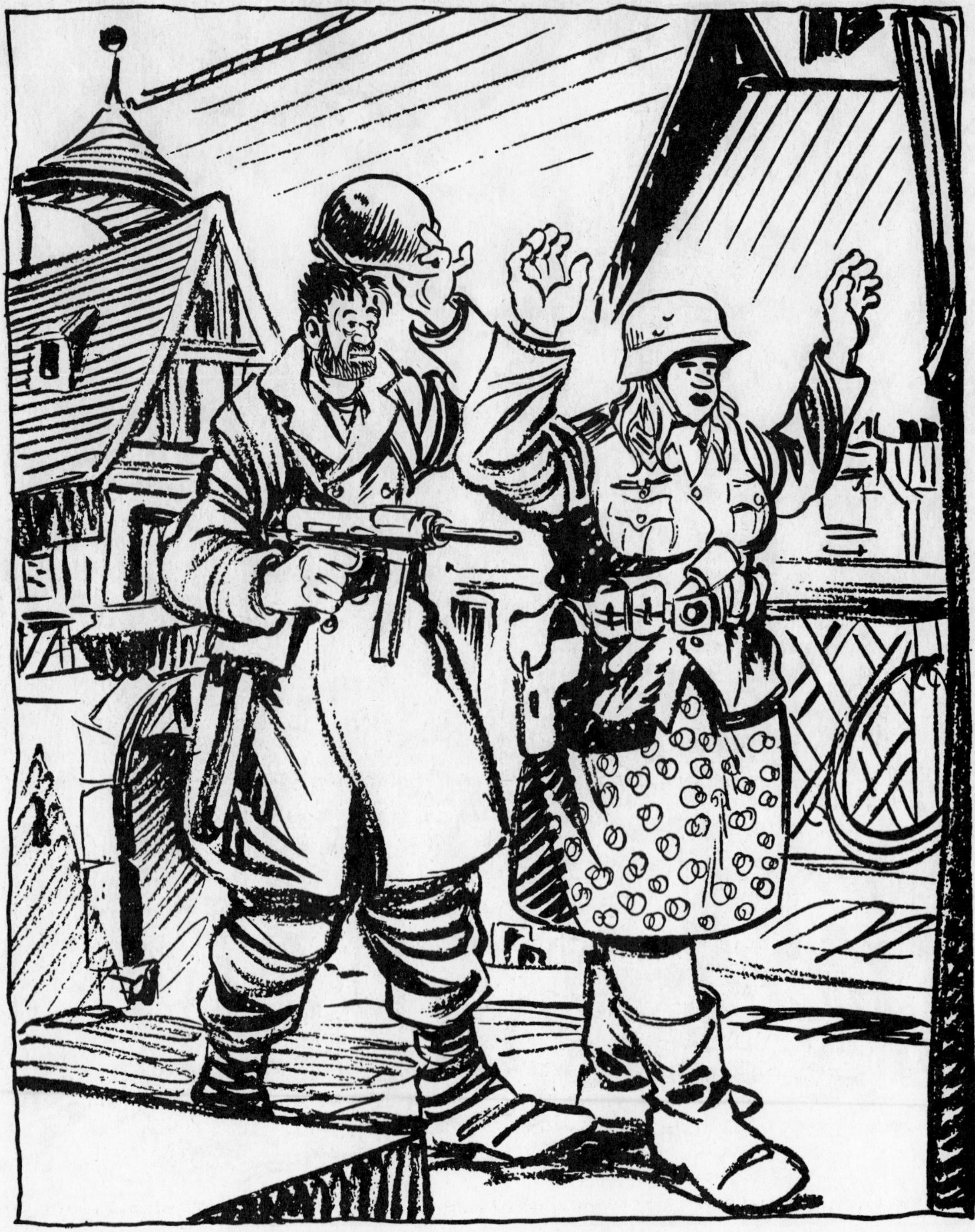

The perfect gentleman

"Don't look at me, lady. I didn't do it."

"Did ya ever see so many furriners, Joe?"

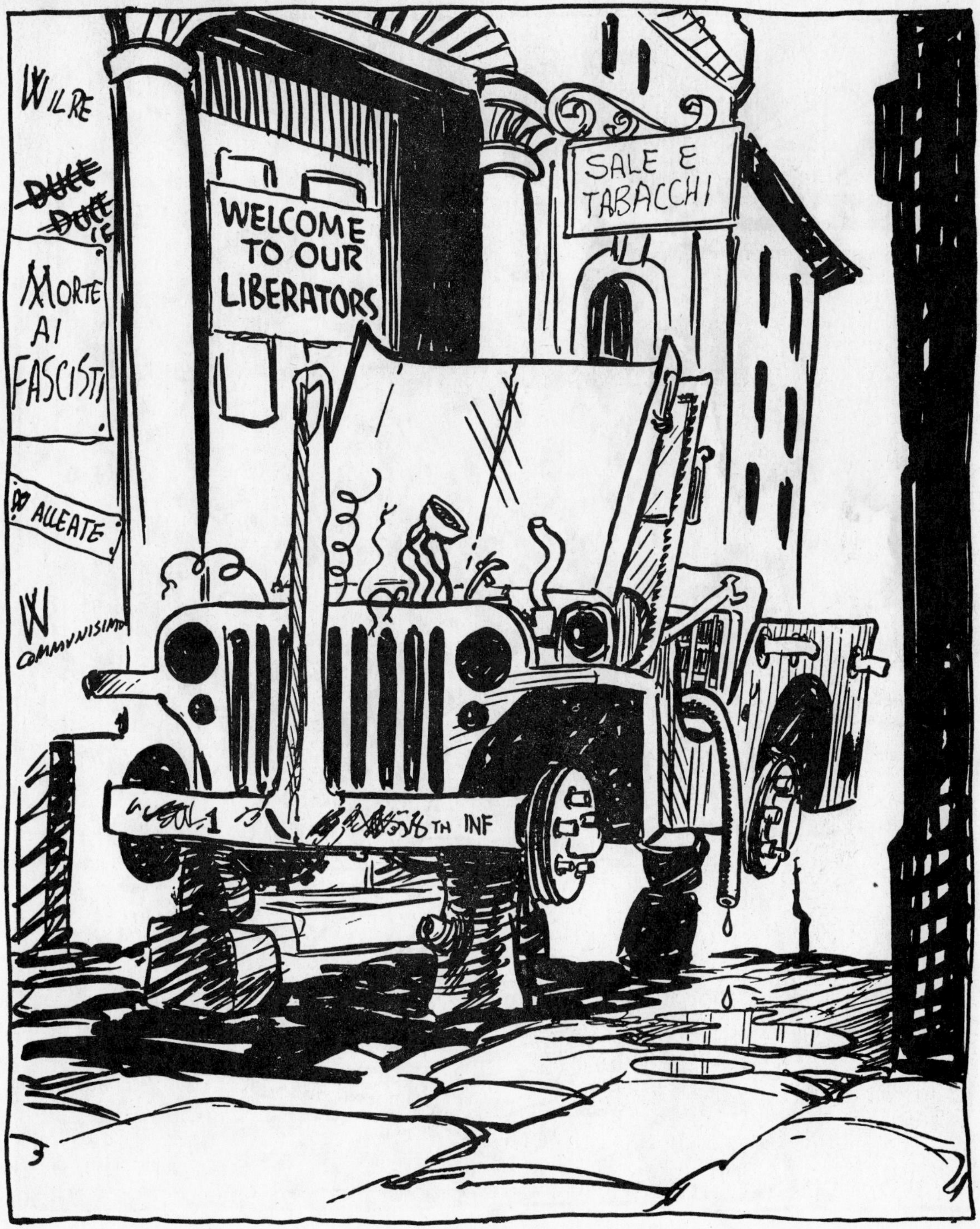

W IL RE
Morte AI FASCISTI
ALLEATE
W COMMUNISIMO
WELCOME TO OUR LIBERATORS
SALE E TABACCHI
TH INF

"This is th' town my pappy told me about."

"I am waiting to see what hatches."

"We oughta tell 'em th' whole Army don't look like us, Joe."

"Wisht somebody would tell me there's a Santa Claus."

"We sure got th' goods on this guy, Captain. Civilians wuz supposed to turn in their weapons."

"Has this fruit been washed?"

"Gee, Gertie — th' front!
Wait'll we tell th' magazines
what it's like!"

"*Eet's a food advertisement een an American magazine.*"

"Seen any signs of partisan activity?"

"*Th' doc says it's nothin' serious—just hardened arteries.*"

"Hey, Fritz—how far are the
Russians from Berlin?"

"Hey, Ivan—how far are the
Americans from Berlin?"

"I don't think th' krauts like bein' liberated."

V-E Day

"Th' hell with it. I ain't standin' up till he does!"

"I'm headin' fer th' la-a-ast round-up!"

"Button dot pocket, dummkopf!"

(NOTE: During the confusion following the surrender of the Wehrmacht in Italy, some still-intact German units in Northern towns kept their own armed MP's on duty for several days as the Americans came in.)

"If ya see Willie, tell him Joe's lookin' fer him. He swiped my razor."

"*Pvt. Hodges just completed basic training in the States. He will brush us up on our close-order drill.*"

"Yer combat badge don't count. Ya need more of these battle participation stars."

"Must be worth at least two hunnert points. . . ."

"*. . . an' I raise you 20 de-mobilization points!*"

"*Ya look like one of them war heroes, Joe.*"

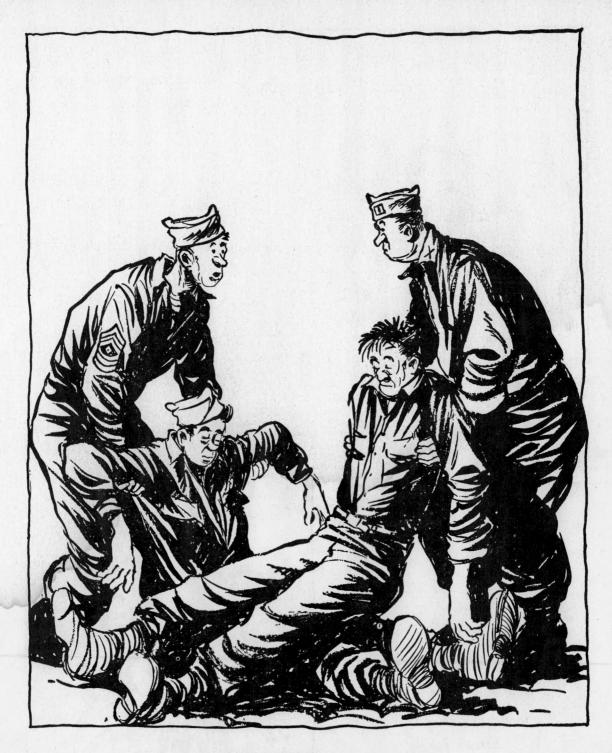

"I see ya told 'em they're goin' home."

"Please try to find her a good home."

"Next question: Do you wish to remain in the army? It says here I gotta ask."

"*I don't remember no delays gittin' us overseas.*"

"*My companion and I find these transatlantic flights very tedious . . .*"

"Ya gotta git rid of him. We don't want this plane involved in no scandals."

"Poor fellers. They ain't heard about th' cigarette shortage..."

"He thinks the food over there was swell. He's glad to be home, but he misses the excitement of battle. You may quote him."

"Two used-car salesmen and three veterans' organization representatives waitin' fer you to come out."

"Essential to th' war effort, Willie. They held up my discharge until th' latrine in barrack 27 is clean."

"My check is seven cents short. I refuse to move until it is corrected."

"*Come to daddy, ya wonderful little 12-point rascal!*"

"Major Wilson! Back in uniform, I see."

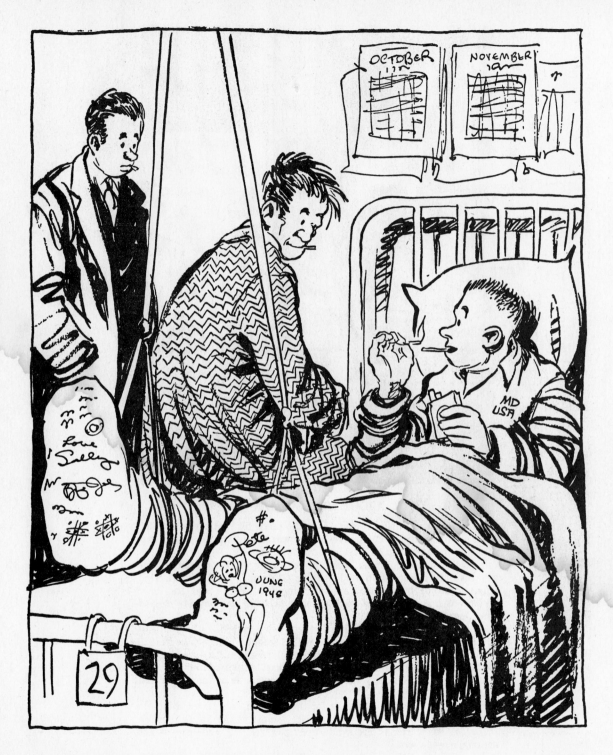

"How's things outside, boys? Am I still a war hero or a drain on th' taxpayer?"

ABOUT BILL MAULDIN

Born on a farm in New Mexico, Mauldin made his first cartoon "sale" to an animal medicine company when he was nine years old, with a cartoon showing a boy and girl crying over a puppy's grave.

From this small beginning, Mauldin went on to win international fame with his pithy comment on the life of the GI during World War II. That famous pair of bedraggled, mud-slopping GIs, Willie and Joe, have become as much a part of the American heritage as Tom Sawyer and Huck Finn.

Mauldin was awarded his first Pulitzer prize in 1945—the youngest person ever to win a Pulitzer. He received his second Pulitzer prize in 1959 for a trenchant cartoon of Boris Pasternak. He was cited by the National Cartoonists Society in 1959 for the best editorial cartoon of that year, and in 1962 won the "Reuben," the Society's top award as cartoonist for that year.

Now a staff editorial cartoonist for the Chicago *Sun-Times*, Mauldin served from 1958 to 1962 as editorial cartoonist at the St. Louis *Post-Dispatch*. His cartoons are syndicated to a reading audience of 250 national newspapers.

He is married to the former Christine Lund and is the father of six sons and a daughter. The Mauldins live in Santa Fe, New Mexico.